Women's Athletics: Coping With Controversy

EDITED BY

Barbara J. Hoepner, Chairman
DGWS Publications
6645 Heather Ridge Way
Oakland, California   94611

The Division for Girls and Women's Sports
of the
American Association for Health, Physical Education,
and Recreation

Women's Athletics
Women's Athletics
Women's Athletics
Women's Athletics
Women's Athletics
Women's Athletics
Women's Athletics

GV
439
A68 / 28,825

aahper
publications

Order from AAHPER Publications-Sales
1201 Sixteenth Street, N.W., Washington, D.C.   20036

PREFACE

For many in attendance, "Women's Athletics" seemed to be the theme of the 1973 AAHPER National Convention in Minneapolis. Even though the official convention theme was "Unity through Diversity," every session I attended somehow commented on woman's role in society and her desire to participate in athletics.

Thus the birth of the idea for this special publication. While it is true that many sessions sponsored by the Division for Girls and Women's Sports naturally centered on the problems of women in athletics, there were other areas that, suprisingly, did so as well. To truly appreciate this phenomonon, one should realize that each session was designed by an individual, usually without consultation with other session planners, and there was only one such session each year. With this understanding, one can see how truly pertinent the topic of "Women's Athletics" is to us today.

The History Area invited Betty Spears to speak on "The Emergence of Sport as Physical Education," and the talk dealt with women's, not men's, sports. The Philosophical and Cultural Area had as their topic, "The Women in Athletics." The speakers, Mimi Murray, Jack Scott, Jan Felshin, and Charlotte West divulged many insights into their experiences in this realm. The National Council of Secondary School Athletic Directors united with the Division of Men's Athletics to study "Women's Rights in Athletics." Marv Helling gave interesting views of a director of a State Interscholastic Athletic League about high school girls playing on "boys'" teams and "girls'" teams. The Therapeutic Council devoted their session to Holly Wilson, one of the few female Certified Athletic Trainers in the U.S., who spoke on women athletic trainers or the needs of female athletes for training personnel and services. The College and University Administrative Council devoted their session to "The Past, Present, and Future of Women's Intercollegiate Athletic Programs." They assembled the people who were most instrumental in the formation and direction of women's collegiate athletics today, Lu Magnusson, Jo Thorpe, Carole Oglesby, and Anita Aldrich.

Our gratitude goes to those area Vice-Presidents and Chairmen-Elect who assembled this fine array of knowledgeable speakers. Women's athletics is a timely topic, the "now" problem for many in athletics. As the role of women in our society is changed, so is their place in athletics changed. This publication includes what is being said about women's athletics by knowledgeable athletes such as Olga Connolly, coaches such as Nell Jackson, and researchers such as Margaret Dunkle and Mary Roland Griffin.

The women athlete, what does she want? Why does she want it? How is she going to get it? These are just a few of the questions answered in this publication.

Barbara J. Hoepner

Contents

Overview:
Women's Rights

Equal Opportunity for Women in Sports

Margaret C. Dunkle

MARGARET C. DUNKLE is a Research Associate
for the Association of American Colleges' Project
on the Status and Education of Women. She follows
the maze of federal legislation that pertains to discrimination against females in athletics and physical
education, and suggests preventive action.

Perhaps all women athletes should be mountain climbers because the plight of women in sports programs is clearly an uphill struggle.

Athletics is a sensitive issue for many people. Athletics both reflect and perpetuate the ideas people often have about what is right for boys to do and what is right for women to do. Sex stereotypes are often deeply ingrained and confronting them head-on can be difficult. Boys are supposed to be strong and aggressive, both physically and emotionally. Women, on the other hand, are supposed to be weak and passive, both physically and emotionally. So the myth goes, and myths die hard.

Often, because these stereotypes or myths are so deeply ingrained, they may even be difficult to identify. When in doubt, a good rule of thumb is to substitute the word "black" for "girl." For example, when "I wouldn't want to compete against a girl" becomes "I wouldn't want to compete against a black," the discrimination becomes obvious. Similarly, "Women don't have what it takes to compete;" "Blacks don't have what it takes to compete." "Nothing is more humiliating than to be beaten by a girl;" "Nothing is more humiliating than to be beaten by a black." "No one will take a woman coach seriously;" "No one will take a black coach seriously." "Women coaches need less pay;" "Black coaches need less pay." When these changes are made, the discrimination sticks out like a sore thumb.

Why aren't women encouraged in athletics? Perhaps, in part at least, because the traits associated with athletic excellence — achievement, aggressiveness, leadership, strength, swiftness, self-confidence — are often seen as being in contradiction with the role of women. For example, a judge in a 1971 Connecticut court case denied women the right to participate on a cross-country team, saying that:

> The present generation of our younger male population has not become so decadent that boys will experience a thrill in defeating girls in running contests, whether the girls be members of their own team or an adversary team. . . . Athletic competition builds character in our boys. We do not need that kind of character in our girls, the women of tomorrow. . . .

Now, women in educational institutions have the same protection against discrimination because of their sex as minority group members do because of their race. Now women in educational institutions, both employees and students, have legal protection against discrimination.

Employment Legislation

In January 1970, when the Women's Equity Action League filed the first charges of sex discrimination against universities and colleges, there were no laws that prohibited sex discrimination against women in education, faculty or students. Only the Executive Order applied, which forbade contractors from discriminating in employment. It was not enforced with regard to discrimination on the basis of sex. Sex guidelines had not been issued, and Order No. 4 which details the requirements for affirmative action plans did not include women; it applied only to minorities. Women have come a long way in the past three years, but there is much still to be done.

The Executive Order forbids all contractors from *discrimination in employment*. It doesn't affect students unless a student is also an employee. It is not law, but a series of rules and regulations that all federal contractors must follow. Its main provision is that it is not enough to stop discriminating; the contractor has to have an *affirmative action plan*. If a contractor doesn't have an acceptable plan, he (and the contractor is usually a "he") can lose money, i.e., federal *contracts*.

Revised Order No. 4 tells a contractor how to set up an affirmative action plan. He needs to do at least the following:
1. Develop a data base on all job classifications.
2. Have a policy statement which forbids discrimination.
3. Appoint a person to be in charge of the program.
4. Examine recruiting, hiring, promotion policies, salaries and other conditions of employment.
5. Identify areas of underutilization and develop specific plans to overcome underutilization.
6. Develop numerical goals and timetables.

Perhaps the most controversial issues are goals and timetables. These are not quota systems. Quota systems keep people out; goals are numerical aims contractors try to achieve. The employer sets goals in line with the number of qualified women available.

What happens if a contractor doesn't meet the goal? If the contractor can show good faith and document his efforts to recruit, hire, and promote women, nothing would happen, for the obligation to meet the goal is not absolute.

There is no intention whatsoever to force employers to hire unqualified women or minorities. If the best qualified person is a white male, that's who is hired. An employer must show good faith, make a genuine effort to recruit women. (Good faith does not mean calling one's white male colleague, asking if he knows a "good guy for the job" and then saying, "I'd have hired a qualified woman if I could have found one.") Also, the employer must use equal criteria; the same standards must be applied to everyone. For example, an employer could not refuse to hire women, but not men, with small children.

Why are universities so upset? They have generally relied on the "old boy" method of recruiting, the vast informal network of old school chums, colleagues and drinking buddies, a network from which women have largely been excluded. To recruit in a different manner means change, and change is never easy, particularly if it means women and minorities coming in to threaten the power base.

Employers in universities have never had to specify criteria for hiring and promotion. Now the Health, Education and Welfare Department (HEW) is asking them to explain why Mr. X is a full professor and Ms. Y is a lecturer, particularly when X hasn't published since he rewrote his thesis and is a terror to the students, while Ms. Y is continually awarded the "best teacher" award and has a string of publications. HEW, incidentally, will not set criteria for institutional hiring and promoting. Rightfully, the institution and/or department heads should set criteria. HEW does ask why someone was hired or not hired, and what the criteria were. If an employer never has had to justify a hiring or promotion decision, this is a pretty threatening thing to be asked. On the other hand, if an administrator can't justify a hiring or salary decision, then either somebody is in the wrong job or getting the wrong salary, or else the institution has an incompetent administrator.

There are rumors flying that affirmative action is dead. Those rumors should be squelched. In Washington there is a lot of rhetoric, but the proof is in the pudding, that is, the budget. The Office for Civil Rights, which enforces the Executive Order, has gotten a $3,000,000 budget increase (which includes about 60 new field positions in the Division of Higher

Education). The Equal Employment Opportunity Commission (which enforces Title VII of the Civil Rights Act of 1964) has received a 45% budget increase. The U. S. Commission on Civil Rights, which received jurisdiction over sex discrimination in 1972, has gotten a 13% increase. J. Stanley Pottinger who, as Director of the Office for Civil Rights, was criticized as being too aggressive, has been promoted to Assistant Attorney General for Civil Rights. Obviously, affirmative action is not dead.

Title VII of the Civil Rights Act of 1964 was amended in March of 1972 to include educational institutions. It forbids discrimination in employment and applies to all educational institutions, regardless of whether they receive federal aid. This includes elementary and secondary schools. Title VII is enforced by the Equal Employment Opportunity Commission which is appointed by the President. Like the Executive Order, individual charges can be filed as well as charges of a *pattern* of discrimination.

Unlike the Executive Order, no affirmative action is required; employers are required to not discriminate in employment. The Executive Order, in contrast, requires affirmative action plans of all contractors with contracts of $50,000 and 50 employees, regardless of whether charges have been filed. Under the Executive Order, reviews can be conducted without charges being filed; indeed, if a contract is a million dollars or more, there *must* be a review before it is awarded. Under Title VII, on the other hand, generally there are no investigations unless charges have been filed.

Should conciliation fail, the Equal Employment Opportunity Commission can take an employer to court. This is a new provision which strengthens EEOC's hand. It ought to speed up the conciliation process considerably. Currently, EEOC has a huge backlog, and it can sometimes take a year or two before an investigation is even started. (Unfortunately, HEW is similarly backlogged).

In the Education Amendments Act (Higher Education Act), effective July 1972, is a little noted section that extends coverage of the Equal Pay Act of 1963 to executive, administrative and professional employees, including all faculty.

The question many people ask is: "If unequal pay on the basis of sex is already forbidden by the Executive Order, by Title VII, and by Title IX of the Education Amendments Act of 1972, why is the Equal Pay Act so important?"

12

The Equal Pay Act is important not because of what it does, but because of *how* it does what it does. It is enforced by the Wage and Hour Division of the Employment Standards Administration of the Department of Labor. It was the first sex discrimination legislation enacted, and it has been successful in getting women millions of dollars in back pay.

One of the major advantages of the Equal Pay Act is that its complaint procedure is very informal. Also, unlike Title VII and the Executive Order, under which the individual complainant's name is generally revealed to the employer, the complainant's name is not revealed to the employer under the Equal Pay Act. In fact, an employer may not even know that his establishment has been reported to be in violation of the statute. Reviews can be conducted whether or not a complaint has been reported. Moreover, when a review is conducted, it is almost always of the entire establishment. After a review is conducted, the employer may be asked to settle on the spot if a violation is found, i.e., raise the wages of the underpaid workers and pay back pay to them. The statute of limitations is two years for a non-willful violation, three years for a willful violation. Should the employer refuse, the Department of Labor can go to court. In the past, 95% of the cases were settled without court action.

Currently, there is virtually no backlog in equal pay cases, although this is expected to change as word of the Act gets out to academic women.

What does this plethora of legislation mean to women in athletics and physical education? It means that a woman physical education teacher cannot legally be paid less than a male teacher who does substantially the same work. It means that, for all employment purposes, the physical disability related to pregnancy and childbirth (as opposed to child rearing) must be treated like any other temporary disability such as gall bladder, prostate or hernia surgery.

It means that retirement benefits must be the same regardless of sex. At present, a woman receives lower monthly benefits upon retirement than' a man with an identical employment and salary record because, on an actuarial basis, the woman is expected to live longer.

It means that anti-nepotism rules, which virtually always limit the career of the wife, are illegal.

It means that male coaches cannot legally be paid more than female coaches. The discrepancy may take the form of a reduced teaching load, release time, or extra duty pay for male, but not female, coaches. For example, in a 1972 issue of the Washington *Post*, an article described a local school board conflict over $270,000 budgeted for extra duty pay for coaches for boys' teams and $20,000 budgeted for coaches for women's teams. A school official quite seriously suggested that, "If the . . . $20,000 for extra duty pay for girls' programs were cut and went *back* to the male coaches, that might be the difference in negotiations." A few years ago this type of action would have been legal; no more.

If institutions practice this sort of sex differentiation or discrimination, they are subject to government intervention and court suits which could conceivably yield hefty settlements for back pay and damages. Federal money can be withheld or taken back, and institutions can be debarred from receiving federal money in the future.

But laws don't enforce themselves. Increasingly, advocacy groups, such as the Women's Equity Action League and the National Organization for Women, as well as campus groups, are filing complaints against colleges and universities for discriminatory practices against both women employees and women students.

Educational Legislation

Concerning students, Title IX of the Education Amendments Act of 1972 has broad implications for the treatment of women in athletic and sports programs. The key section of Title IX reads:

> No person in the United States shall, on the basis of sex, be excluded from participation in, be denied the benefits of, or be subjected to discrimination under any educational program or activity receiving federal financial assistance. . . .

All educational institutions which receive any federal money, including money received via revenue sharing, are covered by this law. Although there are some exemptions from non-discriminatory admissions, this law requires all educational institutions to provide equal opportunities to their students, regardless of sex, once they are admitted.

Title IX of the Education Amendments is patterned after Title VI of the Civil Rights Act of 1964 which prohibits discrimination against the beneficiaries of programs receiving federal money on the basis of race, color and national origin, but not sex. Like Title VI, Title IX is enforced by the Office for Civil Rights of the Department of Health, Education and Welfare. It provides students with the legal tool to protest sex discrimination. It is a potentially powerful tool: if an institution does not comply with its provisions, the government may delay money, take back money previously awarded to the institution, or debar the institution from receiving future contracts or grants. Although implementing regulations have not yet been issued, the law is in force. Complaints can be made by writing to HEW Secretary Weinberger.

Title IX has implications for a variety of issues — admissions, the awarding of fellowships and financial aid, equal job opportunities for female and male students, flexible programming and part-time opportunities, sex-stereotyping in textbooks and the curriculum, the equalization of student rules which are different for women and men, sex-typed counseling, honorary societies which admit one sex only, women's studies programs, and so forth. The primary concern here is the impact Title IX will have on sports and athletic programs.

The time, energy and money that are spent on athletic opportunities and facilities for men, but not women, are coming under increasing scrutiny and criticism. Although there are some honest disagreements over what constitutes equality in terms of sports and athletics, there is no question that, whatever the definition, women do not receive an equal opportunity in this area in virtually every educational institution in the country.

The inequities in terms of money alone are tremendous. For example, women at a "Big Ten" university had to have bake sales and sell Christmas trees in order to finance their athletic activities. At one state university with an annual budget for the male athletic teams of approximately $800,000, the women had difficulty getting $15,000 to finance their athletic activities. The women at one Ivy League institution had to sell candy bars, have bake sales, find "free" coaches, and rent out space on their team bus to support their activities. They did get some money from the college, however: they were funded on a par with the Chess Club.

Collegiate Compliance with the Law

What must an institution do to be in compliance with the law? It must have a *clear policy of nondiscrimination in athletics*. It must provide equal athletic opportunity regardless of sex. This includes nondiscrimination in: the adequacy and accessibility of facilities and equipment; the athletic opportunities and teams available; opportunities for interscholastic competition (including comparable accommodations); coaching and physical education staff; scholarship opportunities; admission to courses (such as coaching courses); and institutional media coverage.

Before considering these items in detail, it would be helpful to mention one point: the government is interested in *equality*. It is not interested in itself determining or mandating the philosophy or practices of sports or athletic programs. This rightly is the prerogative of those in athletics. But, once a philosophy or a practice is determined, it must apply to women and men equally.

Perhaps the simplest, most direct way to define equality is in terms of money, that is, per capita expenditure by sex. Women students are increasingly questioning such "standard" or commonplace practices as routinely using the doctors and facilities in the campus infirmary for boys', but not women's teams. Similarly, they are questioning health services which regularly treat a football player's torn ligament but do not provide routine gynecological services for women. Women are questioning the fairness of budgeting which funds the male sports off the top, but forces the women's sports to compete with "clubs" for funding from student government.

For example, at one state college in Utah, the women were funded through the student government, while the boys received financial support directly from the student budget. The student government initially told the women that "they wouldn't support a bunch of girl jocks;" they did finally get a budget of $300.

Increasingly, women on campus are becoming angry about this sort of discrepancy. Increasingly, women on campus are wondering why they should subsidize male athletics. There is now serious talk on some campuses to encourage female students to withhold part of their student activity fee to protest these inequities in athletics.

The adequacy and accessibility of facilities and equipment. Often now the facilities which women may use are second-rate, if they exist at all, and/or they must be used at off hours — during meals, before sunrise, late at night, or between three and six A.M. Just as black schools used to get the leftovers from the white schools, so do women still get the leftover athletic equipment and facilities from boys. The story of the new gym going to the boys' teams, while the old gym is routinely "retired" to women's sports is almost too commonplace to mention.

This sort of routine relegation of women to the second-rate facilities is illegal.

The athletic opportunities and teams available. At present, team opportunities for women are much more limited than those for boys. For example, until Massachusetts passed a state law allowing high school girls to participate in any non-contact boys' varsity sport (if the sport was not offered separately for girls), boys' sports outnumbered those for women by two to one.

Under Title IX, however, there is no legal justification for differentiating between contact and non-contact sports. If, for example, a woman is qualified to play on the football team, it looks as if Title IX will give her that right. Of course, few women will qualify, just as few men qualify.

There has been no difference of opinion over whether fully qualified women can participate in all sports, contact or otherwise. The question that has been "sticky" is whether two "equal" teams can be allowed (the "separate but equal" principle), or whether all teams must be coeducational, or whether some combination is allowable. It is not clear how HEW will handle this issue. What some groups are asking for is that, in some instances, two teams, one primarily for women and one primarily for men, *may* be allowed provided there is equal treatment, facilities, etc., and provided that people of either sex, when of appropriate height and weight, are able to play on the opposite team.

The Women's Equity Action League has issued the following statement on athletic opportunities for women:

> In terms of athletic programs . . . the thrust of efforts to bring about equal opportunity for women must be two-fold: While outstanding female athletes should not be excluded from competition because their schools provide teams only for males, separate but equal programs should also be provided for average female students, who cannot compete equally in athletics with male students.

The whole question of "separate but equal" is sticky, in large part because there is such a long-standing, although admittedly not proud, tradition in athletics of "separate but unequal" for women and men.

The problem revolves around equality. If, for example, an institution agreed to admit women to all its teams and then funded only varsity basketball, football and heavyweight wrestling, it would not be complying with either the letter or the spirit of Title IX. There is, in the employment legislation, a firmly established principle that, even though a policy or practice may be fair on its face, it is in violation of the law if it has a disparate impact or discriminatory effect on an affected class — in this case, women.

Opportunities for interscholastic competition. The norm now is for the boys' teams to go first class and for the women's teams to go at a cut rate, to pay their own way, or not to go at all. For example, women at one Ivy League institution were forced to pay their own way and take taxis to a game. Commented one competitor, "There's nothing that hurts team spirit like a taxi." There is no question that this blatantly unequal treatment is in violation of Title IX.

Coaching and physical education staff. Students must have an equal opportunity to be taught by or coached by competent staff, just as staff members must be hired, promoted and paid without regard to their reproductive organs. At least one woman, Bettye Jean Bennett of Memphis State University, has dreams of being a football coach. Her route may yet be rocky, but at least the legal barriers have been removed.

Women often have fewer physical education teachers and coaches, and these few receive lower salaries and have heavier teaching loads than do men teachers. This is sex discrimination against both the women teachers as employees and against the women students, and this discrimination makes an institution vulnerable to the almighty wrath of four laws: Title VII of the Civil Rights Act of 1964, the Equal Pay Act, the Executive Order, and Title IX of the Education Amendments Act of 1972.

Scholarship opportunities. Under Title IX, women and men have to be eligible for scholarships on the same basis. This is a change from the present situation. A recent poll of member institutions in the Association for Intercollegiate Athletics for Women showed that 80% favored a change in the Division of Girls and Women's Sports' position forbidding scholarships for women students and that, in fact, the ruling is in the process of being changed.

Legally, it doesn't matter whether institutions give athletic scholarships. What does matter is that they do the same thing for both sexes.

18

Often the argument used against women's athletics is that they are not money-making propositions. It is common knowledge that, at most institutions, football is not a money-making operation. And even at those few "big football" schools that claim to make a profit, one cannot help but ask if the institution is truly making a profit when it subsidizes the stadium, provides "free" (via the student health service) medical care to the teams, pays the coaches' salaries and absorbs countless other costs. It is yet to be argued that men's swimming, baseball and track teams should be abandoned just because they don't have huge gate receipts. Clearly, when someone presents this sort of financial flim-flam, they are saying more about what they think about women than what they think about money.

It should be noted also that the fact that something makes a profit doesn't make it legal.

Clearly, the double standard abounds in athletics. Women athletes are often regarded as biological misfits or mutations, while male athletes are revered as "real men." Women athletes are often regarded as cute little things who decorate the gym, while boy athletes are hailed as "the leaders of tomorrow."

Myths die hard. But times are changing. The double standard is on its way out. Women have found out that they like exercise. And women have found out that rocking the boat is much better exercise than rocking the cradle.

Women's Rights in Athletics

Marvin Helling

MARVIN HELLING is the Associate Executive
Director of the Minnesota State High School Athletic
League.

The philosophy of the Minnesota State High School League is of fundamental importance in regard to the girls and boys in interscholastic athletics under its guidance.

The purpose of interschool athletic competition is to provide an educational experience outside that of the immediate curricular institution. It is well-understood and documented that the human body requires a diet of activity and nutrition to enable it to reach total development. Nowhere is a concept proposed that the human male needs activity more than does the female. Both benefit equally from the physical and psychological effects of physical activity.

Physiological capabilities, however, do differ in specific areas such as muscle mass, cardiorespiratory endurance, and the ability to utilize oxygen for energy formation. The most highly skilled and highly trained girls can, and in some instances do, surpass the performance of boys, particularly those who are in the lower range. But, the performance range of highly skilled boys extends much higher than the girls. This range is true in random samples from normal population as well as in highly competitive athletes.

The League believes that it is not educationally sound to provide open-team membership as opposed to separate teams for boys and girls. The results of such a policy will have little effect on the existing teams established for boys. It will, however, have a devastating effect on the competitive opportunities available to girls.

It further believes that *female athletes deserve, and have a right to, an athletic program in which they not only have an opportunity to participate, but also have an opportunity to achieve and be recognized for their ability.* All League efforts have been to develop separate interscholastic teams for boys and girls.

In regard to legal rights, the courts generally have held that state high school associations are voluntary associations, and the courts will not interfere unless rules are illegal or arbitrary, unreasonable, and capricious. There have been few successful challenges, especially on the appeals level. Courts generally have been reluctant to interfere with the discretion of school officials.

Many states have statutes which authorize establishment of local associations by providing that school boards may delegate authority to such an association.

Morrison vs. Roberts 1938 is quoted as follows:

> Surely the schools themselves should know better than anyone else the rules under which they want to compete with each other in athletic events . . . and if the officials of the various high schools desire to maintain membership in the association, and to vest final rule enforcement and authority in the Board of Control, then so far as affects the affairs of the association, the courts should not interfere.

In the past, courts have affirmed that participation in interscholastic activities is a privilege (not a right protected by the Constitution).

What about girls on boys' teams? There is no consistency in rulings. Some support separate programs; others not. Both state and federal courts have been involved, charging violation of the equal protection clause of the Fourteenth Amendment of the U.S. Constitution.

Courts generally have preferred to ignore total repercussions, (i.e., boys on girls' teams, girls on contact sport teams, girls on boys' teams, even when the school sponsors a girls' team, etc.) and to focus on one girl or a select group of girls. *This privilege is not possible for educators who must be concerned for all.* Recent court decisions in Minnesota have declared that *League rules providing separate athletic programs for boys and girls discriminate against females in violation of the Equal Protection Clause of the Fourteenth Amendment.* The League does not support this limited perspective, but has suspended the rules to provide time for study of the long-range effects of the open-team concept.

The League continues to be concerned for the welfare of the 200,000 boys and 200,000 girls in the secondary schools of Minnesota. 140,000 boys and 60,000 girls are presently participating in the separate athletic programs in Minnesota. It is projected that there will be a participation of 100,000 girls by 1975.

The League is confident that local boards of education will continue in their efforts to provide equal sports programs for girls and boys. The open-team concept will not accommodate the thousands of girls who desire to participate in athletic programs. It is recognized, even by the courts, that the girls will have little impact on the teams developed for boys. The highly skilled girl on the boys' team may find little opportunity for recognition and achievement for her class of performance.

During the past year in Minnesota, three girls competing in four sports were declared exceptions to the League rule of separate programs. They were highly skilled and highly trained girls, each with a national and/or state ranking by a non-school athletic association. Their amount of participation is significant as a forecast of the open-team membership concept:

Tennis Player: She played in four high-school dual matches against fifth- and sixth-seeded opponents. She lost the first two matches and won the last two matches. She was defeated by a teammate and did not earn a berth on the school team.

Cross-Country Track: The boys' athletic rules provide that participants may compete on only one team during that season; she chose not to compete with the boys' team and participated in AAU girls' cross-country meets.

Cross-Country Skier: She skied on the high-school boys' cross-country team at the beginning of the season. She was invited to become a member of the U.S. Women's Cross-Country Ski Team and left the boys' school team during the middle of the season.

Slalom Skier: She has a national ranking of 92 in girls' skiing; ranks third in Minnesota. She participated in one boys' meet and placed eighteenth among about 60 entries. She was not selected for the team to go to the State Skiing Meet.

These girls are "exceptions." They are not representative of the "average" high school girl; and yet, they encountered limited opportunity as participants on the boys' athletic teams. Recognition for their ability and level of achievement had to be sought outside of the high school athletic program. Is this to be the fate of the many thousands of high school girls who desire to compete in athletics? It must not be so.

As school boards face the dilemma of increasing costs and lowered budgets, they must make difficult decisions about their athletic programs. They may, however, better respond to the needs of their total school population through separate athletic programs for girls and boys than propose the elimination of one-half of the participants. Such a proposal cannot be justified under a label of ending discrimination for girls in athletics.

Future policy and future rules and regulations may not come from the educators, but rather from court decisions.

What finally becomes *women's rights in athletics* may well be the result of court decisions — decisions based on educators' power of, or lack of power of, persuasion as they represent their association's philosophy in the courts.

While the educator is busy in his environment, the courts may be responding to: special interest groups in hot pursuit of their selfish goals; over-zealous parents seeking an additional gift for an already gifted daughter; a talented girl using the free legal counsel available for the fun of it, (it's exciting, and puts down the establishment); the girl who would rather win one more medal, one more ribbon or one more match, rather than win the big one which would be a victory for all of the girls who want a program.

Should this be the type of persuasion that determines the destiny of women's rights in athletics?

What about the colleges and universities that allow women on men's teams? This kind of leadership is no different than the small town that finds it cheaper to let one girl play on a boys' team than suffer the expense of providing opportunities for all girls. It is the easy way out. It is hard to believe that women who consider themselves high in the collegiate academic world would tolerate this kind of compromise.

Additional problems are created by the non-school teams and organizations. Today, there is a fantastic growth in non-school organizations, all competing for the services of the best athletes. These organizations are active in swimming, wrestling, skiing, tennis, hockey, etc. They depend on many educators for their very existence. They use school and university coaches to provide teaching skills, access to school-owned athletic facilities, and managerial skills in administrating contests, meets, and tournaments. Few educators can wear two hats and not let their priorities get mixed up.

Many naive school coaches, athletic directors, and even school boards have fallen prey to the non-school organization that offers to be the feeder program for the school team. This appears to be a money-saving program. Remember, if part of a program is mortgaged out, there is the risk of having the mortgage foreclosed. This happens when: non-school organizations use their influence to replace a school coach, director, or even a superintendent; non-school organizations seek to fill school board positions with people sympathetic to their philosophy; non-school organizations challenge the very roots of the school and college programs as they use the legislatures and the courts to guarantee their right to use the school athletes during the school year and even during the school's sports season.

Isn't it strange that none of these so-called amateur organizations have come to the defense of the separate-program concept in the schools and colleges, while half of their very existence depends on separate male and female competition? Separation is the life-blood of the various amateur organizations; however, they could care less for the problems created in the schools while they stand in line waiting to claim the athletes trained by the schools.

Educators interested in doing something to enhance programs for girls should seek opportunities to get involved. The tragic story comes to mind of the girl who was raped in a subway station while numbers of people passed by, and no one responded to the girl's cries, "Help me! Help me!" It's hard to believe that all of those people had valid reasons for not wanting to help. The reasons that they might have offered might be very close to the rationale that many educators lean on as they go their busy ways and let pass the opportunity to make a worthwhile contribution to their profession:

"I don't think it's serious."

"She asked for it — probably just another 'libber.' "

"Must hurry home to my family."

"This comes at a bad time, I'm very busy; otherwise, I'd help."

"I don't want any publicity; might hurt my image."

"Someone should survey these things and find out what should have been done."

"I'd rather write a paper on the psychology of the affair than get involved in the problem."

"Someone else will help. That will solve the problem, and I will not have to get involved."

That's right. Others will get involved. They will make the decisions that determine future policies.

Again, when, where, and how do educators get involved? First there must be a commitment to the programs that are believed to be educationally sound and a determination to have a voice in the (legal) decisions made. Second, educators must start to compete, to get into the game and make themselves known; make contributions to the cause; actively support those who are in the arena and make things happen. (It must be recognized that each person is either a part of the problem or a part of the answer.) Third, each educator must be a doer: testify in the courts; write letters to people who count; give speeches on behalf of school athletic programs; hold conferences to enlighten people where misunderstandings exist; publish papers; start and support programs for girls. Respond to the cries: "Help me! Help me!"

The Emergence of Women in Sport

Betty Spears

BETTY SPEARS, from Wellesley College and
The University of Massachusetts, is a noted historian
and authority in synchronized swimming.

By 1900 sport was well on the way to becoming the central focus in
college women's physical education programs. Information on the emergence
of sport in women's physical education classes is meager. The familiar
textbooks present clearly the development of gymnastics, but picture hazily
the unfolding of sport in women's programs. Discussions of intercollegiate
athletics either exclude women or give them only scant treatment. Some
authors imply that the only role of women in sport was to share the men's
interests. The early curricula are described in gymnastics, with sport as an
unofficial peripheral activity. Most authors place the change from
gymnastics to sport after 1910. They credit the students with the impetus
for athletic sport. However, facts disclosed in primary sources present a
very different history from that in the literature. The period from 1875 to
1910 was a time of major developments in higher education for women
and in physical education. Data from twenty institutions have been analyzed
according to three periods and according to four types of institutions.[1]
The first period, reaching back to the founding of Oberlin College in 1833
and extending to 1890, examines the role of sport in the beginnings of
women's higher education. The second period, from 1891 to 1900, establishes
sport instruction as an integral part of the physical education curriculum.
The third period, from 1901 to 1910, documents the complete acceptance
of sport as the dominant component in physical education for college
women.

The colleges and universities cooperating in this study represent four
types of institutions which were admitting women during the period of the
study: private women's colleges, private coeducational institutions, state
universities and state normal schools. These institutions were selected on
the basis of a 1903 article by Hanna plus a few hunches as to the availability
of data. Of the twenty reporting, six were, and still are, private women's
colleges. Three were private coeducational institutions, one of which was
a normal school of physical education. Four were state universities, and the
remaining seven, state normal schools, two of which opened as women's
colleges. Only in the first period dealing with the founding and early
programs of the institutions did the type of institution significantly affect
sport development. Therefore, the data in that period are divided according
to type of institution.

---

[1] See Appendix

1833-1890

In this first period, sport played a special role in the founding of women's colleges. At that time there was great resistance to the idea of higher education for women. Two major objections were raised. First, women were mentally inferior to men. Second, they were physically unable to stand the rigors of college level study and daily classes. After all, delicacy was the accepted life style for women. Fashion designers, clergymen, physicians and journalists fostered this image. Victorian women were described as delicate, not by nature, but by design. Corsets, tightly laced to achieve tiny wasp waists, bustles, hoops and yards of trailing skirts prevented most, if not all, physical activity. These delicate women were expected to remain indoors and pursue such feminine pastimes as embroidery and painting on glass. They accepted ill health as their lot. Every month women had "the vapors" or were otherwise indisposed. Matthew Vassar characterized the feminine image of the period as a "style of feminine beauty (which) . . . too often blooms but palely for a languid or a suffering life, if not for an early tomb." (1) Somehow, this upper-class image ignored the sturdy farm girls, the workers who toiled long hours in the factories, the secretaries with their twelve-hour day and the average woman who kept house and raised a family.

Opponents of women's education argued that "to demand of women the same hours and continuity that men give to college work, is a physiological insult." (2) Contemporary sources showed 45% of women suffered from menstrual cramps, and another 20% suffered from assorted ills. Thus, for physiological reasons, 65% of the women would require the college program to be adjusted for them. Also, it was reported that overstudy would give the girls brain fever. They would be weak and unable to have children.

When Matthew Vassar and, later, Henry Fowle Durant wished to provide education for women equal to that of men, they first had to demonstrate the mental and physical capacity of these inferior females. To prove the physical capacity of the female, a carefully conceived plan was followed. A lady physician was appointed to watch over the health of the young women. She taught courses in hygiene, physiology and anatomy. Exercises were conducted regularly. Special costumes, shorter and looser than daytime dresses, were worn for exercise. Each day the students were required to spend time out of doors. And sport equipment was provided. Participation was encouraged or, perhaps, required. Sport for women, then, was initiated as part of the larger plan to produce healthy young females capable of engaging in higher education.

In 1865, Vassar explained his beliefs in physical education. "Good health is essential to the successful prosecution of study. In the education of women, this is a consideration of peculiar importance . . . because of the peculiar delicacy of their physical organization, rendering it specially liable to derangement from neglect or misuse." (3) He planned a special School of Physical Training to give instruction in riding, flower-gardening, swimming, boating, skating and "other physical accomplishments suitable for ladies to acquire, and promotive of bodily strength and grace." (4) The school, housed in the Calisthenium, contained the Riding School, gymnasium, and bowling alleys.

Ten years later when Henry Fowle Durant founded Wellesley College he followed Vassar's pattern. Believing that young women could do their best mental work only if it were balanced by physical activity, Durant stressed the importance of vigorous exercise. The one building, College Hall, included a gymnasium and was located near the lake on the new campus. Durant bought boats for rowing in the fall and spring. He encouraged ice skating in the winter. Unable to purchase tennis equipment in this country, he imported it from England.

Goucher, founded in 1885, followed a pattern similar to Wellesley. Gymnastics were taught. Sport facilities were available and participation encouraged. Mount Holyoke, which retained its seminary name until 1892, insisted on calisthenics to to improve grace of motion. A daily walk of one mile and domestic work supplemented the exercise program. Sophia Smith provided for a college which would be suited to the mental and physical wants of women. She did not wish to render "her sex any the less feminine, but to develop it fully as may be the powers of womanhood." (5) Although Smith College announced regular exercise in the gymnasium and in the open air, sport was not suggested to develop or maintain vigor.

Other than the Brooklyn Normal School of Gymnastics, the private coed institutions, the universities, and the normal schools did not arrange special sport programs at the time of their foundings. Neither did they use sport as a means of gaining physical vigor for their students. Founded by Anderson in 1886, the Brooklyn Normal School of Gymnastics, however, taught both gymnastics and sport from the beginning. During Oberlin's early years, the students engaged in popular recreational sports such as croquet and bicycling. Stanford University's founder built two gymnasiums, one for women and one for men. There was to be no discrimination between the sexes. However, the founders expected only about a dozen women to enroll. He was surprised when almost 200 applied on the first day. The 200 women shared Stanford's two tennis courts with the men.

In 1873, after 25 years of controversy, women became full-fleged students at the University of Wisconsin. A gymnasium had been fitted up in Ladies Hall, but for sport, the students relied on their own resources. Shortly after the University of Nebraska opened in 1871, the students organized informal activities. Founded in 1876, the University of Oregon struggled to survive. For almost two decades, no provision was made for women to exercise. In fact, Oregon's first president forbade the students "to attend skating rinks, public dances, and dancing clubs during the session." (6) At the same time he expressed concern for the possible adverse effects of the students' sedentary and scholarly lives. At the University of California in Berkeley, physical education for men began in 1871, but no regular classes for women were offered until 1886.

Of the five coed normal schools submitting data, four were founded between 1866 and 1876 as a result of state legislation for teacher preparation. Neither gymnastics nor sport appear to have been considered by their first administrators. Over 25 years later, North Carolina still questioned educating women at the state's expense. In 1889, one impassioned supporter of a women's normal school wrote the state assembly:

> Why is it that for a hundred years the State has been helping the stronger and letting the weaker take care of themselves? Shall the state help her sons to develop their intellectual and industrial power and do absolutely nothing for those who are to be the mothers of the next generation of men? These girls, and those of coming generations . . . are doomed to live and drudge and die without having known the blessings of being independent. (7)

When the Woman's College at Greensboro did open in 1892, it followed, somewhat, the pattern set by other women's colleges. A lady physician instructed students concerning hygiene, bathing, and other personal matters. To promote student health and strength, calisthenics were taught. Sports were not provided nor encouraged.

Vassar College, Mills, Arnold, West Chester and Wellesley taught sport during this period. Mills and Vassar taught horseback riding in 1864 and 1866 respectively. Mills reported archery instruction. Arnold, the professional normal school, offered fencing, swimming, rowing, games and athletics. Wellesley taught crew and bicycling by 1890, and West Chester listed instruction in walking and bowling. The first instance of sport in the physical education curriculum involving large numbers of students occurred at Vassar College.[2] In 1876, from November to April, gymnastics were required, but from April to June of that year, the students selected a game or sport in place of gymnastics. Many students selected more than one game. This is the first clue to the popularity of sport and games as compared to gymnastics.

Sports also were introduced for recreation and required exercise. Croquet, archery, tennis, ice skating and bowling were introduced before 1880. Goucher opened its swimming pool in 1889. Wellesley organized a tricycle club. Again, the women's colleges provided more sports and provided them earlier. The University of California's football club was an exception. Football was not reported by any other school. The ladies did play. According to the school yearbook, their "fair forms could often be seen through the evening haze, like fairies at their capers." (8)

Prior to 1890 few faculty were appointed in physical education or related subjects. Most of the faculty were engaged by the women's colleges to teach gymnastics, but, before long, they were involved in sport. Anderson at the Brooklyn Normal School of Gymnastics became an early leader in physical education. When Hanna was appointed at Oberlin, she initiated improvements in the women's program as well as a physical education major.

Three important developments occurred in the first period of this study. First, Vassar and Durant recognized sport as a means of attaining physical vigor which was essential for the success of their women's colleges. Second, the students at the private coed institutions, the universities, and the normal schools enjoyed sport as casual recreation. Third, some colleges, for example Vassar, taught sport and incorporated it into their physical education curriculums.

Contrary to physical education literature which reports that sport was developed by students before a place was found for it in the curriculum, Vassar, Wellesley, and Goucher included sport in their initial plans. The philosophy and financial resources of the founders, as well as the

---

[2] See Appendix

geographical location of the schools, undoubtedly affected the selection of the sports offered. Vassar College and Wellesley, both on New England lakes, encouraged rowing and ice skating. Vassar College began horseback riding, and Wellesley, tennis, both elite sports. Tennis was eventually played by all schools. Just how sport moved from school to school is not known, but it would make an interesting study. By the end of the first period, in 1890, fourteen sports, from walking to football, had been introduced to the twenty institutions reporting. Also, one can recognize isolated instances of sport instruction in the physical education program.

One additional point should be made about this first period. Matthew Vassar understood and suggested values of sport other than health. Although health was his underlying reason for including sport in the college program, he believed feminine sports should be appealing to students. Further, he thought riding, boating, swimming and skating promoted grace as well as strength.

1891-1900

The second period was characterized by a frenzy of sport activity resulting in the adoption of sport in the physical education curriculum. In general, gymnasiums and athletic facilities were built. More faculty were appointed. The sport program increased in size and scope. Team games were invented and imported. Dress reform made vigorous sport possible. Sport instruction became an accepted responsibility of the department of physical education. Students were active in sport and, on many campuses, controlled recreational sport.

Throughout this decade colleges and universities built gymnasiums, tennis courts, and athletic fields. West Chester opened a splendid new facility. Dr. and Mrs. Ehringer were in charge and devised an "equal opportunity program." On Tuesdays, Thursdays, and alternate Fridays the women used the gymnasium from 8:00 A.M. to 3:15 P.M. From 4:00 P.M. to 6:00 P.M. the men occupied the building. On Mondays, Wednesdays, and alternate Fridays this plan was reversed.

When the institutions could not provide sport facilities, sometimes the students did. For example, in 1882, a tennis court was built by the young ladies at the University of Wisconsin. At Wellesley, the class of 1894 raised money for a new boat house. The Greensboro girls cleared and prepared the grounds for basketball and cricket. These student contributions to facilities were a discernible indication of their sport enthusiasm.

The inventions, first of basketball, and then of volleyball, plus the importation of English field hockey made a great impact on sport programs for women. Senda Berenson, who had the geographical advantage of being close to Springfield and the beginnings of basketball, introduced the game to Smith in 1892. Both Berenson and the students liked the quick, spirited game. Basketball incorporated the beneficial results of gymnastics with the excitement and interest of competitive sport. Basketball could be played both outdoors and indoors. With the large rooms provided for gymnasiums, and improved lighting indoors to make it possible, basketball was a boon to sport lovers. It caught on immediately and spread across the United States. By 1894 the University of Oregon played basketball. Actually, Hoepner reported basketball at Berkeley in 1891. It is not necessarily presumed to be the same as Naismith's game. When volleyball was invented in 1896, it too, found its way into the women's programs, but was never as popular as basketball.

Although 1901 usually is the date assigned to the introduction of field hockey in the United States, Goucher played the game in 1897. Miss Flyborg, the Assistant Director of Athletics at Goucher, studied English outdoor games and found cricket and hockey suited to girls. She told a reporter from the *Baltimore News American*, "If played scientifically, the girls need not be rough, and there is a little more skill required than in basketball. The girls will wear tennis skirts and shoes. It is a good cold-weather game, and is as interesting on grass as on ice." (9)

The new games either were modified for women or introduced as women's sports. The students were enthusiastic about them and even suggested including basketball in the required exercise class. The idea of groups of women playing against other groups of women must have startled many people in the nineties. The phenomenon of team sports in the women's programs should be explored in more detail than is possible at this time.

A number of other sports were added to the curriculum and to the recreational program. Mount Holyoke taught track and field, and so did Nebraska. Smith and Winthrop played cricket. Wellesley introduced golf and lacrosse. Fencing was popular and taught in several schools. Mount Holyoke enjoyed rinkle polo. Although basquette, tetherball and croquet have disappeared from the curriculum, the sport offerings in college physical education in the last decade of the nineteenth century reveal the framework of our present day traditional curriculum.

The means by which sport became incorporated into the curriculum varied from institution to institution. Vassar College continued its practice of games in the spring. In 1895, twenty teams of basketball were organized after the Easter holiday. At Wisconsin, in the fall and spring, students substituted two hours of club participation in place of gymnastics. There were clubs in golf, bird, bicycling, rowing, tennis and bowling. Struma and Remley report that, with the exception of crew, each club had a woman instructor assigned to it. Crew had a man advisor.

In 1891, Oberlin permitted exercises for diversion after the student had completed her prescribed gymnastics. Battle-dore, shuttlecock and ring toss were listed among the possible diversions. By 1897-98, Oberlin required daily activities for two years. During the student's first year, she could exercise out of doors one day a week, if her pulley weight examination had been passed. In the spring, if her participation card was worked up to maximum time and weight, the student could devote one day per week to games, and two days a week to out-of-door exercise. Clearly, sport was making inroads on the gymnastics programs.

At Wellesley, Hill conducted an experiment with students in gymnastics and crew to determine if crew produced the same physical improvement as gymnastics. Sixty students participated in the 1893 experiment. Twenty students received lessons in scientific oarsmanship for five months and rowed on the lake for one month; twenty received training in Swedish gymnastics for five months; and, as in all proper experiments, there were twenty students who received no physical training for five months. Measurements taken at the beginning and end of the experiment included girth of chest, capacity of lungs, strength of chest, strength of back, depth of chest and breadth of shoulders. Needless to say, the measurements of students receiving no physical training demonstrated no improvement, and in some cases, decreased. Gymnastic students gained more in lung capacity, but overall the rowers held their own. Here was statistical evidence that students could improve and maintain their physical vigor through sport.

By 1895, students at Wellesley could apply for admission to training classes in sport. In that year, 153 freshmen applied, and 71 were admitted to crew, 21 to basketball, and 16 to golf. In addition, 134 upperclassmen were in sports that year. President Shafer of Wellesley enthusiastically reported:

33

> Out-of-door sports . . . are made to serve a larger and higher purpose
> than ever before. Steps have been taken to reorganize the college
> boating with this new object in view. The Director of the Gymnasium
> gives each crew two lessons per week in scientific oarsmanship. . . .
> Crews are no longer selected because of their vocal talent, but because
> of their general physical fitness. (10)

For several years prior to this time, members of Wellesley's crews had been
selected because of their ability to sing. The crews rowed and serenaded
from the boats. But no longer. Now they were taught scientific oarsmanship.

In some institutions, non-physical education faculty taught sport. In 1894,
a former student at the University of Nebraska, while a member of the
English department, played, coached and managed the girls' varsity
basketball team. In 1896, swimming lessons could be obtained at Smith
from some of the college girls.

By 1900 then, an irreversible trend had begun, away from gymnastics and
calisthenics, and toward sport as the legitimate content of the instructional
program. Interacting events and influences provoked the change. Hill's
experiment with crew and gymnastics demonstrated that sport could be
substituted for exercise without adverse effects on the students' health.
At Smith and Vassar Colleges, student enthusiasm for gymnastics waned.
Smith introduced competition in the annual gymnastics drill to make it
more exciting for the students. In 1893, after Easter, only fifty percent of
the Vassar seniors attended gymnastics regularly. According to Ballintine,
these older students tended to absent themselves without excuses. The
Vassar seniors were cutting gym. The advent of team sports increased the
students' growing disenchantment with gymnastics. In contrast to the thrills
of basketball, calisthenics were dull. Evans' basketball research affirms
student boredom and lack of interest in gymnastics. She alleged that
instructors used games in their classes as "sugar coated pills with which
to force down more strenuous gymnastics work." (11)

Undoubtedly the students were happier with sport than with gymnastics.
Probably the faculty were happier. One may ask, "Did the faculty, realizing
the students' attitude, seek an acceptable alternate to gymnastics? Did the
faculty substitute sport for gymnastics to appease the students? In the
1890's, were the faculty trying to 'save the requirement?' Did the faculty
enjoy teaching sport more than gymnastics?" While ostensibly health
remained the primary reason for requiring exercise, perhaps the faculty
were not completely honest with themselves. Maybe they liked to teach

sport. Therefore, they offered sport. Do teachers, today, offer sport because they enjoy teaching it, but mask their enjoyment in educational jargon they believe is acceptable to administrators?

During this second period, students played an important role in recreational sport. As noted previously, they sometimes obtained courts and fields which the administration had not been able to provide. Students also managed facilities. At Oberlin, the newly formed Young Women's Tennis Association took charge of two tennis courts. Sports clubs were popular, especially in the universities. California established a tennis club. Wisconsin boasted seven sports clubs during this period. Intercollegiate basketball began. The *Philadelphia Press* reported that the Anderson women played the Sargent women "in a hair pulling contest under the guise of a basketball game." (12)

While students played a prominent role in the conduct of recreational sports, the faculty were responsible for the growth and expansion of the programs. Sport was firmly under the direction of the department of physical education. Berenson of Smith, Ballintine of Vassar College, and Hill of Wellesley were active in promoting sport. Berenson not only introduced basketball to Smith, but adapted the rules to women. Ballintine introduced many sports to Vassar. Hill not only experimented with crew and gymnastics, but supported a variety of sports in Wellesley's program. Goucher appointed instructors from England who introduced field hockey to the students. Hanna and Anderson continued to develop professional curriculums. When Anderson moved the Brooklyn Normal School of Gymnastics to New Haven, more extensive facilities made an expanded sport program possible.

By 1900, at the close of the second period, sport instruction was an integral part of many physical education programs. From an administrative viewpoint, increased facilities and staff made the emphasis on sport possible. Gymnasiums were built, fields and tennis courts installed, and golf courses constructed. It was a time of growth. Physical education faculty, especially in the women's colleges, accepted the responsibility for several different aspects of the program. Required gymnastics, sport instruction, recreational clubs and intercollegiate games came under their supervision. Not only were the antecedents of our present day curriculum apparent in the nineties, but also our present day responsibilities were taking shape.

The most important development of the nineties was the increased enthusiasm for sport and the decreased interest in gymnastics. More research is needed to determine the reasons and attitudes behind this change. If President Shafer of Wellesley was an example, the trend to sport was approved by the administration. If faculties approved curriculum and requirements then as now, they, too, must have approved the new approach. The advent of team sports, dress reform and better facilities also influenced the assimilation of sport in physical education. The second period in this study, the last decade of the nineteenth century, was distinguished by the rapid development of sport in women's physical education and the integration of sport into the instructional program.

1901-1910

In the last period, the first decade of the twentieth century, sport was finally accepted. The curriculum became sport oriented. Announcements of sport courses appeared in catalogues. Efforts were made to organize and regulate sport. Underlying the acceptance of sport in physical education were attempts to examine sport on its own merit rather than as a means to an end.

The instructional program grew. More and more, sport was identified as physical education. Each institution in the study submitted data indicating sport offerings. By 1910, in over half of the departments of physical education reporting, sport had become the central focus in the curriculum. Instead of sport being disguised as part of a gymnastics course, sport names appeared in the catalogues.

In 1901, Applebee demonstrated field hockey at the Harvard Summer School of Physical Education. At Ballintine's invitation, she visited Vassar that fall, and then toured the other New England women's colleges teaching field hockey. In 1902, the Iowa State Normal School offered tennis, hockey, and golf classes to women. Mills taught fencing, field hockey, indoor baseball and volleyball. Oregon students played tennis. Mount Holyoke organized a basketball class. In the early part of the decade, Wellesley offered sport courses called recreative training. The instructors in these courses were assisted by the officers of the organized sports. The object of this program was "to furnish a *moderate amount* of healthful physical recreation to the *greatest number of individuals*." (13) Wisconsin permitted students to elect systematic courses in sport as soon as they attained the minimum standards of vigor, development, and skills. Systematic courses included a variety of sports. Within the requirement, Wisconsin insisted that students be able to swim fifty yards.

Gymnasiums continued to be constructed, but, in some institutions physical educators pleaded in vain for additional facilities. In 1908 Hanna wrote:

> We need a swimming pool for the thousand young women who are here. Swimming is probably the best allround physical exercise; it develops courage and coordination, gives control of the breathing, and strengthens the muscles. Every one should be able to help himself or others in case of necessity. (14)

At Vassar, the problem of regulating team sports concerned Ballintine. In 1901, she reported that she had persuaded the students, "somewhat against their will," to form house teams rather than class teams in hockey. This was done to prevent too intense feeling and excitement. After the students complained about the officiating and roughness, basketball also had to be regulated by the department. Ballintine insisted that the only way to control the game was to supervise it. However, she pointed out to the president of the college that these arrangements made more work for the members of the department.

The Winthrop teachers also supervised athletics and outdoor activities. Organized teams existed in volleyball, captain ball, tether ball, basketball, and tennis. Students submitted records showing one-half hour daily vigorous exercise. Checking the records was a responsibility of the Director of Physical Training. Not all efforts at regulating and supervising women's sports were successful. The March 7, 1904 *University of Oregon Weekly* reported the basketball game between the freshmen and sophomore women:

> Perhaps the most jocular and altogether most novel feature of the game was that a number of college men, in order to meet the requirements necessary for admittance . . . attired themselves in women's clothes, veiled their faces and entered . . . Not until the end of the game was it made evident that the women had been outwitted. (15)

Values of sport other than health began to be explored by physical educators. Ballintine stressed the students' needs for recreation and relaxation. Hanna ascribed gaining courage from learning to swim. At a conference of the American Physical Education Association, Gertrude Dudley of the University of Chicago spoke of the values of athletics for later social and professional success. When challenged by Berenson, she admitted she had spoken of athletics only because the subject had been assigned to her. Other authors wished to enhance bodily beauty and grace. Hill approved strong beautiful bodies for both use and ornament. Emphasizing health as the underlying principle, she stressed the importance of joyousness in exercise and of awakening girls to the "delights of athletics."

The final decade in the study, then, was characterized by the acceptance of sport in physical education. Sports were offered as courses and listed in college catalogues. Sport requirements, such as swimming, were instituted. Efforts were made to organize and regulate sport. Finally, values of sport other than health were recognized.

During the thirty-five years covered in this study, sport for women who did not attend college largely paralleled the increasing interest of college women in sport. Croquet was popular with this group just as it was with the college students. Long skirts and tight bodices did not hamper the players. They simply lifted their skirts at the appropriate moment. The fact that both men and women played croquet was an added attraction. Also, the Fencer's Club of New York held classes for women. On the opening day of the Staten Island Ladies' Athletic Club in 1877, the women played dart games, archery and tennis. Tennis, introduced in the mid-1870's, immediately became popular with upperclass women. Some ladies delighted in bathing. Bowling and roller skating were enjoyed. By the end of the period, skilled women players were not uncommon. The major difference between sports for the non-college and college women were the vigorous team sports so dear to the college girls' hearts. They did not gain wide acceptance outside colleges and universities. Certainly, in both educational institutions and everyday society, sport for women gained a larger acceptance.

Sport participation was part of the strife for women's rights in the same crucial period. Women worked for equal legal and employment status. They fought for higher education. They campaigned for the vote. And they sought the right to physical freedom — to health, freedom of movement, and enjoyment of exercise and sport. The place of sport in women's struggle for physical freedom needs to be thoroughly studied. Any aspect of this investigation could be repeated with a larger sample. However, based on the data submitted, four tentative conclusions can be suggested:

1. Sport in higher education was initiated by some of the founders of some of the women's colleges for the express purpose of increasing and maintaining the physical vigor of the students. Physical vigor

was necessary for college women to prove the physical ability of women to engage in higher education.

2. By 1900, an irreversible trend from gymnastics and calisthenics to sport as the legitimate content of physical education had begun. The faculty, especially in the women's colleges, initiated the trend to sport.

3. Before 1910, sport had emerged as the dominant component in the physical education curriculum in many institutions.

4. Health as the rationale for physical education persisted at least until 1910. Values of sport other than health were expressed, but were neither emphasized nor widely accepted.

Sport, initiated to supplement gymnastics in the plan to produce healthy young females, gained interest while gymnastics lost interest. When a young Vassar teacher in 1876 substituted games for exercises, the change had begun. Almost twenty years later, an ingenious experiment provided the evidence that sport could obtain physical results comparable to that of gymnastics. Gymnasiums, playing fields, tennis courts, boat houses and golf courses were constructed. Faculty introduced the new team sports. Both faculty and students liked the sports. There was no turning back. A philosophical rationale for sport other than for health began. By the first decade of the twentieth century, it was clear that sport had emerged as the central focus in college women's physical education. Those "inferior" females who prompted Vassar and Durant to initiate sport for college women really started something.

REFERENCES

1. *Prospectus of Vassar Female College.* New York: Alvord, 1865, p. 4.
2. Van DeWarker, Ely, M.D. *Women's Unfitness for Higher Education.* New York: The Grafton Press, 1903, p. 72.
3. *Prospectus of the Vassar Female College.* New York: Alvord, 1865, p. 3, 4.
4. *Ibid.* New York: Alvord, 1865, p. 5.
5. Sophia Smith's will as reported by Patricia Sullivan, Smith College.
6. *Report of President Johnson to the Board of Regents,* University of Oregon, Eugene, Oregon, June 17, 1886.
7. *The North Carolina State Normal and Industrial College Decennial,* 1902, p. 6.
8. *The Blue and Gold,* Vol. IV, No. 1, published by the Class of 1878, University of California, 1877, p. 4.
9. *The Baltimore News American,* December 6, 1897.

10. Shafer, Helen. *The President's Report,* Wellesley College, 1893, p. 12.
11. Evans, Virginia L. *The Formative Years of Women's College Basketball in Five Selected Colleges, 1880-1917,* unpublished master's thesis, University of Maryland, 1971.
12. *Philadelphia Press,* April 2, 1896.
13. "Arrangement of Courses," unpublished material, Edith Hemenway Eustis Library, Wellesley College, c. 1903-1906.
14. Hanna, Delphine. *Annual Report of the President and Treasurer of Oberlin,* 1907-08, p. 289.
15. *The University of Oregon Weekly,* March 7, 1904, p. 1.

Appendix 1

PARTICIPATING INSTITUTIONS

Private Women's Colleges

Goucher College	Maryland
Mills College	California
Mount Holyoke College	Massachusetts
Smith College	Massachusetts
Vassar College	New York
Wellesley College	Massachusetts

Private Coed Institutions

Arnold College	Connecticut
(Brooklyn Normal School of Gymnastics)	
Oberlin College	Ohio
Stanford University	California

State Universities

University of Wisconsin
University of Nebraska
University of California, Berkeley
University of Oregon

Normal Schools
   Coed:

Central Michigan University	Michigan
State University of New York	
College at Cortland	New York
Towson State College	Maryland
University of Northern Iowa	Iowa
West Chester State College	Pennsylvania

   Women:

University of North Carolina	North Carolina
Winthrop College	South Carolina

Appendix 2

VASSAR STUDENT GAME REGISTRATION *
1876-77

Gymnastics
(November 13-April 13)
Number registered in gymnastics classes   270

Games
(April 23-June 2 or 27)

Ball	25
Boating	94
Croquet	108
Gardening	24
Walking	116
	367**

* Tappan, Lilian, *Report to the President*, 1877, unpublished material, Vassar College, Poughkeepsie, New York.

** Many students selected more than one game.

From Glide to Stride: Significant Events in a Century of American Women's Sport

Richard A. Swanson

RICHARD A. SWANSON is Coordinator of Professional Education in the Division of Health and Physical Education at Wayne State University in Detroit. This paper was presented at the DGWS National Coaches Conference held at Western Michigan University in September, 1973.

In February, 1874, Miss Mary E. Outerbridge, a young society girl from Staten Island, New York, confounded the customs officials at the port of New York by presenting for entry a strange assortment of nets, rackets and balls. Having no previous encounter with such paraphernalia, the officials were at first suspicious and were hesistant to allow the pretty young woman, returning from a holiday in Bermuda, to continue with her odd package since they didn't know how much duty to charge. However, they eventually concurred that the materials were innocent enough and posed no threat to the security of the nation. Thus, the implements for the game of Sphairistike, or Lawn Tennis, were introduced to America, duty free at that.

In 1973, Billie Jean King is one of the best-known names in American athletics. As the highest paid female professional athlete in history, and as the most outspoken and colorful of the present period, Mrs. King is a fitting symbol for women's athletics in America at the threshhold of its second century.

It may strike some as ironic that a woman introduced tennis to this country and that, a century later, it is a woman tennis player who is helping to raise the consciousness level of all women toward the acceptability of sport participation. Social attitudes toward female athletic endeavors have changed slowly and sometimes imperceptibly over the century separating Outerbridge and King. A measure of the cumulative effect of such attitudinal weathering, is the fact that top-flight play by both men and women amateurs and professionals is contributing to the fantastic current growth in the popularity of tennis. Perhaps the myth of the male world of sport can finally be laid to rest and this will be the dawn of an age of sport for humans.

Whatever the age to come, the past has been marked by change, which has in turn been brought on by periodic significant events or movements. It is the purpose of this presentation to examine four such milestones in the past one hundred years of women's sport in America. The four chosen for this study are not claimed to be all-inclusive or the four most significant events. However, those included here are assuredly among the most important in terms of their effect on women's sport in the United States.

The Safety Bicycle[1]

The first event focusing attention on woman's right to partake in healthful, outdoor, physical activity was the development of the safety bicycle in the mid-1880's. Prior to this date, cycling was restricted primarily to those who could afford the $100 to $150 machine, who had the courage and desire to sit astride the steel steed which had a front wheel diameter that varied from forty to sixty inches, and who could don clothing appropriate to safe riding and yet which met the social standards of the day. Naturally then, bicycle riding was mainly a pastime of the upper- and upper-middle class male segment of the population. The introduction of the safety bicycle with its two lower wheels and easier control opened the activity to many additional people, and, with the addition of the drop frame, women began to be numbered among the select.

Important as these technical innovations were, however, the greatest obstacle to putting women on wheels was the social pressure of proper feminine behavior. Momentous decisions had to be made regarding the appropriateness or inappropriateness of the relatively new bloomers for cyclienes, the amount of ankle that might be properly shown or the absolutely rock-bottom number of under-skirts that could be worn. This was in addition to such earthshaking questions as, ". . . should a gentleman cycling down a path in Central Park greet a young bicyclette when they encountered each other?" and, "when was it proper for a young lady to request assistance from a passing male?"[2]

The resolution of these problems did not occur overnight. There were, however, numerous "authorities" who were not at all hesitant about jumping into the fray. For instance, one writer for *Harper's Weekly* offered the judgment that ". . . While it was entirely proper for a strange gentleman to help a lady in distress when he encountered her on the path, a real lady would immediately take her bicycle to the nearest repair shop if one were handy,

---

1. For much of the material on the influence of the safety bicycle, the writer is greatly indebted to the work of Dr. Robert A. Smith which appears in his delightful new book, *A Social History of the Bicycle* (New York: American Heritage Press, 1972).

2. Smith, p. 77.

and not stand along the road waiting for a helpful male to pass." [3]
Continuing, he stated, "There is no more reason for a man cyclist touching
his hat to a passing woman cyclist with whom he is not acquainted, than for
a man riding, driving or walking. Different situations do not alter the laws
of good manners." [4]

The major assault, however, was made on clothing. Amelia Bloomer had
tried mightily in the 1850's to change clothing styles for women. Catharine
Beecher, from the 1820's to the Civil War, likewise advocated looser and
more functional garb which would allow for greater freedom of movement
and less constriction of the circulatory system. These, plus other voices in
the wilderness, however, were not particularly successful in their efforts.
By the era of the bicycle, the average woman was still "burdened by
whalebone- and-canvas corsets that pinched out the 'hour-glass figure' so
beloved at the time." [5] The dress material was heavy, cumbersome and
swept the floor. Needless to say, this was not functional cycling wear. But,
what preaching and writing in an earlier day could not perform, the
two-wheeled chariot did. In 1885, the wife of the president of the League
of American Wheelmen blasted those who would recommend
knickerbockers for women riding a tricycle. She contended that they were
awkward, unnecessary, and unfeminine. She did concede, however, that
while any ordinary dress was acceptable, good sense dictated restricting
the number of underskirts to as few as possible.

With the introduction of the safety bicycle two years later, it became
obvious that this lady's advice was far too conservative. By 1890, women
cyclists were wearing dresses without corsets, as well as blouse and skirt
outfits. A writer in *Outing* magazine suggested shortening the skirts in the
rear to avoid entanglement in the spokes of the wheel while riding or the
pedal when mounting. She did concede, however, that it might be proper
to sew a few lead weights in the front hem as a precaution against the
wind. [6] By 1894, a large number of New York women were wearing bloomers
and other pant-type outfits when cycling. Professor Robert A. Smith, in
his *A Social History of the Bicycle*, reports that by 1895, bloomers had
become so common that they no longer had the attractions of the *outré*. [7]

---

3. Cited in Smith, pp. 77, 78.
4. *Ibid.*
5. *Ibid.*, p. 97.
6. *Outing* (June, 1892), p. 59 and (February, 1892), p. 96, as cited in Smith, p. 98.
7. Smith, p. 101.

Eventually, the bloomer and the shortened skirt moved out of the gymnasium and off the bicycle to affect everyday costuming.

By far, the greatest contribution of the bicycle to the woman of the late nineteenth century was in the relative freedom of movement which it presented to her. In the past, independent travel for a woman was difficult, to say the least. While in the city, public and private coach travel was available, it certainly did not give one a feeling of individual, independent movement. One had to wait upon a scheduled run for public transportation and, at any rate, to depend upon horsepower for private coach. Distant travel on foot was out of the question because of the dress code of the day. For the small town or rural woman, the options were even less.

Enter the bicycle! Suddenly it was possible for a person to move at a speed equal to, or greater than, that of a horse and entirely under one's own power. For men it was invigorating. For women, it was absolutely revolutionary. As the *Minneapolis Tribune* saw it: "Cycling is fast bringing about this change of feeling regarding woman and her capabilities. A woman awheel is an independent creature, free to go whither she will. This, before the advent of the bicycle, was denied her."[8] The freedom was symbolic as well as real. As with Jonathan Livingston Seagull, once you have soared, it is difficult to go back to conventional habits. To the "new woman" of the "Gay Nineties," having once soared, she would not again be forced into the clothes, movement, or ideological corsets of the past. While this had broader social ramifications, it was of special significance to the future role of women in sport and recreation. The gains won on the bicycle would be felt on the gymnasium floor, the track, the pool and the field.

Basketball, The First Team Sport

The second major occurrence in the growth of women's sports is the invention of basketball during the winter of 1891-92. When Dr. Naismith formulated the game that was to be primarily used to keep male athletes at Springfield College in condition during the months separating the football and baseball seasons, he little realized the impact that it would have on women's sport. Within a few months of the first game at the well-known YMCA Training School, women students at Smith College and other eastern institutions were playing it with various modifications. By 1903, Miss Senda

---

8. *Minneapolis Tribune* (March 12, 1894), as cited in Smith, p. 77.

Berenson of Smith could state that, "It is by far the most popular game that women play."[9]

This is not to say that high school and college women were totally void of sport experiences prior to 1891. To the contrary, the 1870's and '80's had seen the introduction of many such activities to campuses across the country, but particularly in the East. Vassar girls were playing baseball in 1876. As one alumna recalled, "The public so far as it knew of our playing, was shocked, but in our retired grounds and protected observation, we continued to play in spite of a censorious public."[10] Somewhat less controversial was the playing of tennis and golf and taking part in formal gymnasium classes devoted to formal gymnastics and calisthenics. Tennis and golf, prior to 1900, were definitely upper-class activities and were played both in and out of schools and colleges. It is reported that sportswomen competed in a tennis tournament in 1887 and a golf tournament in 1896. As early as 1879, twenty ladies joined sixty-nine men in an archery tournament.[11] Again leading the way, Vassar College, under the leadership of Harriet Ballintine, introduced track and field for women in 1896.[12] For the less actively inclined, there was the game of croquet.

Naturally, the costume and prevailing social climate still dictated a leisurely style of play, particularly in tennis. Even basketball, however it was lauded as a "quick, spirited game . . . which cultivated strength and physical endurance,"[13] was somewhat affected by the bulky bloomers and their imitations. In addition, the rule modifications helped to ensure the fact that aggressive movement would be restricted and kept to a minimum. Miss Berenson, for instance, in the first recorded modification for girls in 1894, made the following changes: "(1) a player could hold the ball for three seconds without having it snatched out of her hands; (2) the court was divided into three zones with no crossing from one zone to another; and (3) a player could not bounce the ball more than three times."[14]

9. Senda Berenson, "Editorial," *Basketball for Women* (New York: American Sports Publishing Co., 1903), pp. 7-11, in Aileene S. Lockhart and Betty Spears, Chronicle of American Physical Education (Ed.), (Dubuque, Iowa: Wm. C. Brown Company Publishers, 1972), p. 209.
10. Marjorie Sloan Loggia, "On the Playing Fields of History," *Ms.*, Vol. II, No. 1 (July, 1973), p. 63.
11. Deobold Van Dalen and Bruce Bennett, *A World History of Physical Education,* 2nd edition, (Englewood Cliffs, N.J.: Prentice Hall, Inc., 1971), p. 422.
12. *Ibid.*
13. Berenson, *loc. cit.*
14. Van Dalen and Bennett, *loc. cit.*

In 1899, a Conference of Physical Training was held at Springfield, Massachusetts, and a committee was appointed to investigate the various rules modifications being used by institutions and groups around the country and to draw up standardized rules which ". . . should voice the different modifications used all over the country as much as possible." [15]

The game continued to grow in popularity and, by midway through the first decade of this century, girls were playing for state high school championships in many regions. On the West Coast, in fact, basketball at the college level was considered to be primarily a women's sport until about 1910. Obviously, the game had moved in to fill a void in the overall program of nineteenth-century women's sport. Just as obviously, that void was a lack of team sports. Baseball, by nineteenth-century standards, was too fast. Football was obviously too rough. Field hockey had not yet really caught on. Basketball, then, became the first girl's team sport to achieve widespread acceptance by participants, leaders, and the public.

As more and more girls and young women flocked to the sport, concern began to be voiced regarding the desirability of organized competition for females. As the popularity of the activity increased, press coverage became greater, game crowds became larger, and from time to time there was a lack of what might be termed "wholesome leadership." As Professor Margaret Coffey suggests, "the first seed was planted for the ever-present controversy regarding the extent of sports competition for women." [16] The debate continued through the First World War, and, by 1917, a large body of physical education leaders and interested laymen sought to take control of women's competition in the United States.

Controls of the 1920's

This, then, signaled the third significant event in the recent history of women's sport in this country — the institution of strict controls governing most competition in this country. In 1917, the president of the American Physical Education Association (forerunner of the present AAHPER) appointed a Committee on Women's Athletics to set standards for activities for girls and women. Within five years there were subcommittee on hockey,

---

15. Berenson, *op. cit.*, p. 210.
16. Margaret A. Coffey, "The Sportswoman: Then and Now," *Journal of Health, Physical Education, Recreation,* Vol. 36, No. 2 (February, 1965), p. 39.

swimming, track and field, soccer and basketball. In 1927, it became a
section of the APEA and was known as the Women's Athletic Section.

Also in 1917, Blanche Trilling of the University of Wisconsin, spearheaded
the development of the Athletic Conference of American College Women.
It opposed intercollegiate competition for women and favored girls' rules
for basketball. In addition, it encouraged alignment of the Women's Athletic
Association on each campus with the Department of Physical Education and
likewise fostered student participation in the organization and
administrative aspects of such programs.

A third new agency came into existence in 1923. The Women's Division
of the National Amateur Athletic Federation was headed by Mrs. Herbert
Hoover. It was nearly identical in purpose with the Committee on Women's
Athletics and many of its leaders were active in both organizations.
Membership in the Women's Division was open to either individuals or
groups such as colleges, YMCA's, churches, secondary schools, athletic
associations and women's clubs. While the Division did not conduct or
organize activities, it did seek to promote sport participation among women
and to "establish principles for the wise selection, promotion, and
supervision of women's sports." [17]

These three organizations achieved considerable success in their
objectives. In 1931, Mabel Lee reported that the number of colleges
sponsoring varsity competition throughout the country dropped from 22
percent in 1923 to 12 percent in 1930.[18] The success in eliminating
interscholastic athletics from secondary schools was a good deal less.[19]
At the college level, the play day and sports day became the substitutes for
intercollegiate activities.

A major concern of all three groups was international competition by
women under AAU auspices. The inclusion of women on the 1928 United
States Olympic Team touched off a storm of protest by members of these
organizations. Miss Ethel Perrin, Chairman of the Executive Committee of
the Women's Division of the NAAF, referred to it as a "crisis in girls'

---

17. Van Dalen and Bennett, *op. cit.*, p. 452.
18. Mabel Lee, "The Case For and Against Intercollegiate Athletics for Women and
    the Situation Since 1923," *Research Quarterly,* Vol. II (May, 1931), pp. 93-127.
19. Van Dalen and Bennett, *op. cit.*, p. 453.

athletics." In arguing against the fielding of another team for the 1932 Olympic Games, she stated that the Division could

> . . . only oppose strongly a program that it considers harmful for the girls who may be chosen to train for teams, that requires an enormous expenditure of money and effort in order to produce a huge spectacle of exploitation and that necessarily diverts attention and interest from the sound purpose of athletics for girls — the increased opportunity for physical and mental health and joy for all.[20]

In addition to opposing Olympic participation on the grounds of sports for all, she forwarded the following argument which the reader is free to interpret:

> Girls are not suited for the same athletic programs as boys. The biological difference between them cannot be ignored unless we are willing to sacrifice our school girls on the alter of an Olympic spectacle. Under prolonged and intense physical strain a girl goes to pieces nervously. She is "through" mentally before she is completely depleted physically. With boys, doctors experienced in this problem of athletics maintain the reverse is true. A boy may be physically so weak that he has not strength to "smash a cream puff," but he still has the "will" to play. The fact that a girl's nervous resistance cannot hold out under intensive physical strain is nature's warning. A little more strain and she will be in danger both physically and nervously.[21]

The inability of girls and women to cope was a recurrent theme during this period. In 1933, Agnes Wayman, President of the American Physical Education Association, echoed Miss Perrin:

> External stimuli such as cheering audiences, bands, lights, etc., cause a great response in girls and are apt to upset the endocrine balance. Under emotional stress a girl may easily overdo. There is widespread agreement that girls should not be exposed to extremes of fatigue or strain either emotional or physical. . . . In addition, custom and good taste should always influence in questions of public display, costumes, publicity.[22]

While the efforts of these individuals and groups did not result in the elimination of international competition for American women, it did certainly impede the overall quality of performance at the highest levels.

---

20. Ethel Perrin, "A Crisis in Girls' Athletics," *Sportsmanship*, Vol. I, No. 3 (December, 1928), pp. 10-12, in Lockhart and Spears, *op. cit.*, p. 440.
21. *Ibid.*, p. 441.
22. Cited in Loggia, *op. cit.*, p. 64.

Of course, there were a number of famous women stars in the 1920's, particularly in the acceptable sports of tennis and swimming. But one thinks long and hard to recall the outstanding performers of the '30's and '40's. Beyond Mildred "Babe" Didrikson, the list is sparse. Except for industrial leagues in basketball, softball and bowling, and AAU sponsored activities in these and other sports, there was little opportunity for girls and women to regularly meet top-level competition in this country. More importantly, there existed little opportunity for advanced training for the gifted female athlete unless she chose to, and was allowed to, train with men or unless she could afford private instruction or membership in specialized clubs in swimming, gymnastics, tennis and so forth.

There is no doubt that the vast majority of schools and colleges attempted to offer *basic* instruction and competition to the mass of girls under their direction as per the recommended standards of the watchdog agencies. However, in retrospect, it is also obvious that little or no provision was made for the gifted athlete, or even the average woman who wanted to reach her maximum potential through advanced instruction and competitive experience. The very worthy objectives based upon very real fears and concerns of the controlling groups, while protecting people from over-abuse, at the same time denied large numbers of girls and women over a period of two generations, the opportunity to achieve full actualization. One fears that the baby was thrown out with the bath water and that the tub is only now beginning to be refilled.

Television in the 1960's

The fourth significant event to affect women's sport in the United States is part of the very recent past and of the present moment. From its inception, television has had a love affair with sport. An early experiment in the commercial use of this technological marvel involved the telecasting of a college baseball game. It is certainly not necessary to trace the history of television sports broadcasting to be aware of the importance of TV to sport and vice versa. Until the early 1960's, however, it seems that 99.9 percent of all such telecasts involved male contests. With the exception of the early efforts to telecast the 1952 and 1956 Olympic Games and the exhibitionism of professional wrestling and the roller derby, female athletic events rarely entered the living rooms and taverns of America.

In 1960, however, a strange thing happened. An American woman won three gold medals in track and field at the Olympic Games in Rome.

Now those who were around and were into women's sport prior to the '60's, know what women's track and field in this country was like. The United States was so weak in this sport that it was lucky to find twenty-five or thirty girls to even put in a uniform. After all, Americans didn't want their girls to look like those Russian "Amazons," did they? And everyone knows that all that running, jumping and throwing will make a girl too muscular. And everyone also knows that anyone who excels in that manly sport is a little-bit funny, now don't they? And don't think that these ideas were only held by the uninformed man and woman on the street. There were a lot of women physical educators who felt the same way; who felt that only "ladylike" sports must be promoted. And that meant that the U.S. only played tennis, golf, badminton, swimming, softball, basketball and field hockey. (Now is field hockey more "ladylike" than track and field?) Could it mean that one's own feminity was thus protected?

But, when Wilma Rudolph ran off with all of that gold in Rome, Americans were doubly shocked. First, American girls don't win gold medals in this sport, let alone three of them. Second, Wilma Rudolph was one of the most attractive women to grace American television in the year 1960. That alone destroyed a long-held stereotype. Suddenly, TV discovered women's sport, and the number of televised women's events began to grow, ever so slightly. In 1961, the American Broadcasting Company introduced a weekly program called "Wide World of Sports." This innovative format introduced Americans to a number of little-known athletic events and regularly featured women. In the early and middle sixties, regularly scheduled AAU track and field meets, featuring men and women's events were televised. This was undoubtedly a contributing factor in the fantastic growth of girls' and women's track clubs during this period. Gymnastic and swimming competitions also began to experience broader coverage and hence, more publicity.

Presently, there is nothing approaching equality between the sexes in television sports coverage. The fact that, during this past year, the first national collegiate basketball championships for women could not find a network willing to televise them is significant testimony to that fact. From an historical perspective, however, it is hard to escape the fact that television in the 1960's did, in fact, increase its coverage of women's sport and that at the same time, the latter grew at an unprecedented rate in terms of number of participants, geographical distribution and quality of performance. The acceptance of women's athletics by both women and men in this country has been in large part the result of exposure via television.

This media might be called the greatest agent of social change in the history of the United States. If so, it is hard to believe that the world of sport could be the exception to this fact.

Summary

In conclusion, it might be well to reiterate that it has not been the purpose of this paper to definitively detail all facets of the history of women's sport in the United States. While it is interesting to note that Gertrude Ederle's English Channel swim was accomplished in record time for either sex and to recount all of the championship matches of Helen Wills, it is far more important to understand the broader social conditions and events which have shaped and influenced the American woman's sport experience. While record performances are important in terms of the individual and collective experience of the participants and some spectators, and perhaps contribute to the further acceptance of sport by others, it is also true that these quality performances are perhaps an outcome of the social climate that has been created over a period of time. This social climate is developed by events much broader than the 1945 championship match at Wimbledon, the finals of the three-meter springboard at the 1956 Olympic Games at Melbourne, or perhaps even the outcome of the King-Riggs match of 1973. The events cited in this paper — the safety bicycle, the development of basketball, the controls of the 1920's, '30's, '40's, and '50's, and the influence of television in the 1960's — have had significant and long-range effects on female athletic participation in our society. The identification of other such events in the past, present and future by interested scholars could do much to enlighten those who are a part of the American sport subculture as well as those in the society as a whole. Such enlightenment will, hopefully, have a positive influence on the future growth and development of the sport experience for American women.

Women's Intercollegiate Athletics - Past, Present, Future

Four women who have
played a part in determining
the direction of women's
athletics in this country
provide some insight into
how and why it started,
problems it has encoun-
tered, and directions it has
been forced to take. They
are Lucille Magnusson,
JoAnne Thorpe, Carole
Oglesby, and Anita Aldrich.

The Development of Programs

Lucille Magnusson

LUCILLE MAGNUSSON, from The Pennsylvania
State University, is a Past Chairman of the Division for
Girls and Women's Sports, and was the Chairman and a
Commissioner for the Association for Intercollegiate
Athletics for Women.

The familiarity of each individual with the development of women's
intercollegiate athletics undoubtedly results from one's direct or indirect
involvement. Some individuals observed or coached, and certainly many
have heard tales of the women's basketball games of the early 1920's.
As with many activities at that time, there was no national or local group
concerned with governing and setting standards for these programs and the
participants involved in them. Consequently, some questionable practices
evolved, and many concerns arose about the "exploitation" of the girls and
women. Problems of that era included extensive travel, rowdy spectators,
harsh male coaches and fear of "evils apparent in men's athletics." Beginning
in the twenties, and certainly by the thirties, the philosophy toward varsity-
type competition for women was one of complete disapproval. Competition
in fact became a dirty word. The emphasis shifted to programs for the
masses, "the greatest good for the greatest number," "a girl for every sport,
and a sport for every girl." This philosophy continued in most parts of the
United States through post-World War II days and almost into the 1960's.
Extracurricular sports programs at the college level consisted of intramurals,
playdays, and finally evolved to include sport days.

As with any generalization, there are always exceptions. There were a few
areas of the United States in the South and New England where competitive
opportunities for the girls continued to persist. Gladys Palmer, a brave soul
at Ohio State, had the courage to initiate a national collegiate golf
tournament in 1940. Students seemed interested, and the results didn't seem
too detrimental. After all, golf was a reasonably ladylike sport. With the
exception of the war years, this tournament became an annual event. Before
long it was decided that the location should change each year so that all
areas of the country would have equal opportunity to participate and not
have travel be such a handicap. Shortly afterwards, the "Tri-partite Golf
Committee" was formed to assume responsibilities for this one annual
tournment. This committee had broad responsibilities for the event, the
hostess school, and the standards by which the tournament would be
conducted. As might be suspected, three organizations had representatives
on the committee — Division for Girls and Women's Sports, National
Association for Physical Education of College Women, and Athletic and
Recreation Federation of College Women which, in 1973, changed its name
to College Women in Sports (DGWS, NAPECW, and ARFCW now CWS).

Gradually, questions began to arise relative to competition in sports other than golf and, as a result the National Joint Committee on Extramural Sports for College Women (NJCESCW) was formed by the Tri-partite organizations. The Tri-partite Golf Committee continued to operate under NJCESCW. Events that brought college teams together to compete were being reviewed by the NJCESCW. Also, this Committee established some standards for such events. As time progressed and the 1960's arrived, competition was being looked upon in a slightly more favorable light than in the 1930's. After studying its philosophy and the total sports picture, DGWS recognized that it had, in fact, been discriminating against the highly-skilled female athlete. It was forcing her out of the educational environment to gain competitive athletic experiences, that is, if she were brave enough to pursue such paths and risk the wrath of her instructors. Thus DGWS revised its "Statement on Competition." This and many other developments led to more opportunities for girls to participate in varsity-type programs.

In the mid-1960's, NAPECW, one of the parent organizations of the NJCESCW, voted to dissolve the Joint Committee as did ARFCW. This left a void, and the need for leadership in intercollegiate athletics for women became more apparent. In the meantime, DGWS continued its interest in such programs and developed "Guidelines for Intercollegiate Athletic Programs for Women." Still, no organization existed at the college level to guide and control intercollegiate athletic programs for women. DGWS studied the problems and realized that they had no structure within the Division which could devote the time and attention needed by inter-collegiate athletics. The solution to the problem was the establishment of the Commission for Intercollegiate Athletics for Women (CIAW) as a structure within DGWS. This structure was approved by the AAHPER Board of Directors in the Spring of 1966 and it became operational in September 1967. The initial purposes of the Commission were:

1. To encourage the organization of colleges and universities or organizations of women physical educators to govern intercollegiate competition for women at the local, state or regional levels.
2. To hold DGWS national championships as the need for them became apparent.
3. To sanction closed intercollegiate events in which at least five colleges or universities were participating.

A major concern was to foster the establishment of policy-making bodies at the local or regional levels which would *adopt* the DGWS Guidelines and *enforce* them as policy and, in addition, add other necessary policies. With the help of the NAPECW Research committee, a study was made among the colleges and universities across the United States to determine the need for national championships and the sports in which the need was greatest. In December 1967 Katherine Ley, chairman of CIAW, announced that the Commission would sponsor national championships for college women. Gymnastics and track and field championships were initiated in 1969. The golf tournament fell under the auspices of the Commission from the very beginning of CIAW's operation. There were many problems with which the Commission had to cope. Not the least of these was whether the growth in a given sport should be from the top — that is, with a national champion-ship serving as a motivating factor to participants — or whether the growth should come primarily from the bottom up. The latter assumed that, when there was sufficient competition at the local level, the need for a national championship would emerge. DGWS and CIAW decided that the growth would be most sound if there were encouragement from both the top and bottom of the continuum. Gymnastics presented a somewhat unique situa-tion. There were strong gymnasts spotted across the country, and, unless they competed at the national level, they had little opportunity to know how good they were.

Badminton, Swimming and Diving, and Volleyball DGWS National Championships were initiated in 1970. These national championships have been sponsored annually, and basketball was added to the group in 1972. The growth in competitive sports for the college woman has been both rapid and continuous. It soon became evident that it was impossible to continue national championships on a "you all come" basis. Regional qualifying events are now held in gymnastics, volleyball, and basketball.

With this growth, it became apparent that there was a need for a more structured governing body which would provide leadership and would initiate and maintain standards of excellence in intercollegiate competition for all college women. The Association for Intercollegiate Athletics for Women (AIAW), an institutional membership organization, was designed to fill this need. Memberships were solicited in the 1971-72 academic year, and about 275 schools joined. With an institutional membership organization, each member school assumed the responsibility of maintaining a quality program of women's athletics and adherence to AIAW established policies. The member schools elected AIAW's first officers who assumed the leader-ship of AIAW in July of 1972. AIAW is in its second year as an institutional membership organization, and, to date, the member schools number 367. The philosophy, purposes, and program of AIAW have continued much the same as they were under CIAW since the one organization was a direct outgrowth of the other. There are some very real differences, however, when one recognizes that the member schools are electing their officers each year in AIAW instead of having the leadership appointed by DGWS. Probably even a bigger step is that the member schools vote on all major policy decisions. AIAW is still very much in the growing stages, operating under an interim operating code which was in the hands of each school before it joined. The member schools will hopefully ratify both a Constitution and bylaws in the very near future.

With the support from each member school, all of the officers and committees, and all of the administrators in individual schools, it is hoped that AIAW can help foster the continued growth of sound, quality intercollegiate athletic programs for women. AIAW is committed to athletics in an educational setting, encouraging competitors to be students first and athletes second. This will hopefully result in women athletes selecting a college because it has the quality academic program they wish to pursue as well as a sound athletic program.

The Relationship of DGWS to AIAW

JoAnne Thorpe

JOANNE THORPE, Chairman of the Women's
Physical Education Department at Southern Illinois
University, is a Past Chairman of the Division for Girls
and Women's Sports where she made important decisions
regarding the Association for Intercollegiate Athletics for
Women.

In 1967, the Division for Girls and Women's Sports established the Commission on Intercollegiate Athletics for Women, known as the CIAW. It consisted of three, and later four, women who were commissioned to plan a program of intercollegiate athletics which would include the staging of national championships and which would provide a structure for controlling intercollegiate competition once the initial beginnings were made.

Intercollegiate competition was nothing new to a vast number of college women. At Southern Illinois University, for example, students had competed with students from other universities since the late 1930's and early 1940's. Play was, however, in most cases amateurish and informally organized, while at the same time being quite competitive. Girls are just as competitive as boys, given the same conditions. To label these competitive programs as amateurish is not meant to diminish their appropriateness at the time nor their value to the participants of the times, but rather simply to point up that:

1. The schedules were informally arranged.
2. Travel was not extensive.
3. Events were of a sportsday rather than a tournament organization.
4. The players often coached themselves.
5. The teams often had sponsors rather than coaches per se.
6. The students or even the coaches might officiate.
7. Officials rarely received pay.

DGWS leaders of the early 60's realized that something was indeed missing in competitive opportunities for women. Nationally and internationally, college women were not receiving their fair share of the benefits that young people can receive from participation in a program of high-level competition which is properly planned and controlled.

The CIAW encouraged and gave sanction to the concept of National Championships. The first was held in gymnastics in 1969. Presently championships are held in seven sports: badminton, basketball, golf, gymnastics, swimming, track and field, and volleyball.

CIAW functioned as a standing committee under the DGWS Executive Council for about five years. The program grew, and the responsibilities of the commissioners increased geometrically to the point that a more formally structured organization became a necessity. The institutional membership organization now called the AIAW accepted its first members in October of 1971. Approximately 280 institutions affiliated in the first year. The first elected officers completed their one-year terms of office in June, 1973.

Much dialogue has intervened between the officers of AIAW and the Executive Council of DGWS since the formation of AIAW. With respect to what the relationship of AIAW and DGWS should be, two opposite views have been advanced:

1. That AIAW should separate from DGWS and AAHPER and perhaps merely affiliate with AAHPER more or less as AAHPER affiliates with NEA, or
2. That AIAW should retain a very close tie with DGWS and AAHPER as is the present state of affairs.

These opposite views are not polarized within AIAW or DGWS. There are some AIAW and some DGWS officers who hold both of the points of view.

The present relationship involves an agreement by both groups to the following:

1. Use by AIAW of DGWS rules for all sports in which DGWS publishes rules.
2. Use by AIAW of DGWS officials in all sanctioned events.
3. Adherence by AIAW to DGWS philosophy and standards.
4. Utilization by AIAW of DGWS-AAHPER office support, space, and staff.
5. Utilization by AIAW of liaison relationships of AAHPER with other associations.
6. Submission by the Vice President of DGWS of the AIAW budget for approval of AAHPER.
7. Reciprocal voting privileges of one vote on the other group's executive board or council.

While the present relationship seems to be reasonable and acceptable at this period of time, one must not be so naive as to assume that there will be no pressure for change or that a subject as volatile as intercollegiate competition will ever be associated with the status quo. Those pressures have already been felt and will continue to be felt because the women have dared to follow a pattern of organization different from that example given to them by their male colleagues in the NCAA, NAIA, and NJCAA.

In June of 1971, Walter Byers, Executive Director of the NCAA, began some rumblings which sounded like an interest in getting into the business of women's sports. Suddenly, the NCAA legal counselor had conveniently discovered that the NCAA might be legally liable for not providing sports opportunities for women. Since, according to their constitution NCAA had been authorized to regulate intercollegiate competition and, since at the writing of that constitution, women were only interested in cheering, there was obviously no need to specify "for men." Now that women were getting into sports at a national level, Walter, being the law-abiding person that he is, didn't want to exclude the women. Surely, he had no interest in the television rights or in any monetary gain which might be anticipated from launching a program of sports for women. At any rate, the feelers went out; and several members of DGWS met with Walter and his Women's Committee (on which there are no women and the sex of those on the committee seemed not even to be borderline). Walter suggested that, if AIAW became autonomous and disassociated itself constitutionally from AAHPER, the NCAA might accept it (AIAW) as its affiliated women's organization, but that it would be subject to the constitution and by-laws of NCAA, not equal partners. The real barrier to the marriage was perceived by NCAA to be the problem of being tied to AAHPER. To AIAW and DGWS, it was loss of control and all of that sudden wealth! At any rate, the NCAA counselor was assured that their "divine right to regulate" need not include women, for women have regulated themselves and have managed to survive.

The present relationship which AIAW has with DGWS and AAHPER seems to have several advantages:

1. DGWS and AAHPER have a long tradition of fostering educationally sound programs.

2. DGWS and AAHPER have inspired the highest of professional standards since their inception.

3. AAHPER has been successful in maintaining non-partisan relationships in its liaison functions with allied groups throughout the years.

4. DGWS philosophy, which is essentially that sports should exist for the benefit of the participant, has dominated sports programs for girls and women for the entire twentieth century.

5. DGWS is a standard bearer for girls and women, has their allegiance, and commands a place of almost total and indescribable identity and respect.

While the benefits cited are obviously desirable, the proponents of a separation from AAHPER could probably score some points too. They might claim as advantages of separation the following:

1. AIAW could grow faster without the bureaucracy of AAHPER to detain it.
2. AIAW could become more parallel and consistent with NCAA, NAIA, and NJCAA; and, since it would be the only regulatory group for women, would gain considerable power with these men's groups.
3. AIAW could become more commercialized than the rules of a non-profit educational association such as AAHPER permit.
4. AIAW could lose the baggage of amateurism which lack of funds tends to encourage.

Lest these advantages tend to sound too palatable, there are other considerations to weigh before making a change.

History is important because it may help to anticipate the future. The women of AIAW would be less than intelligent if they did not look at the past with respect to men's intercollegiate athletics in order to draw some inferences about what women's athletics can expect should they take the same course:

1. The Division of Men's Athletics has had as its major thrust since its inception in the 50's to bring athletics back into an educational setting and to improve the professional standards of the leaders of athletic programs. Had these programs been under the influence of AAHPER, it is possible that the need for greater professional standards would never have become the problem that it is.
2. Recently the universities have been tired of NCAA, et al., usurping institutional autonomy. In the final analysis, the institution has complete authority over its students, and institutions are telling that to these regulatory bodies. AIAW should proceed with caution in assuming that any organization outside of the university itself has much authority; probably a professional association would have as much influence as any outside group.
3. It is impossible to legislate allegience. In her twenty years of service to AAHPER, Rachel Bryant built an image for DGWS with which women in the field identify. That image is indestructable, and it perpetuates itself because it was founded upon all of the right things — sports for the value to the participant, a sport for every girl, and always the commitment to standards.

The decision to seek a relationship other than the one which presently exists should be based upon some anticipation of an insurmountable and disproportionate number of advantages of the contemplated arrangement over the present.

Future Directions and Issues

Carole Oglesby

CAROLE OGLESBY, from the University of
Massachusetts, was President of the Association for
Intercollegiate Athletics for Women during 1972-73. She
served as one of the first Commissioners for this
organization, having responsibility for the National
Championships.

The AIAW is at once a product and a producer of the two most
characteristic, frightening, exciting aspects of society: *liberation* and
change. It is child and mother of liberation and change in women's
collegiate athletics.

Looking ahead a decade or more for AIAW, we see multi-problems,
issues, challenges. They are welcomed, for vitality in human development is
nourished best on problem solving and challenge.

There are powerful elements of society now at work to liberate and
improve upon girls' and women's opportunities in the world of sport. A few
of these would be:

1. The Higher Education Act and the Equal Rights Amendment
   translated into action by women's political groups.
2. The expansion occurring in socially accepted aspects of women's
   roles.
3. Media attention finally turning towards women's athletics.

What is the primary challenge which faces AIAW in the midst of this
shifting scene? It is the necessity to resist the temptation to be *passive*
(again) about its own sport experience. "Passivity" is the thoughtless
acceptance of excess and elitism thrust upon AIAW in the guise of "equality"
with some men's programs. Many men's programs do not reflect this dyad
of elitism and excess, but some of them who do are very well known and
seem tempting as models unless evaluated carefully. What is wanted
perhaps is not most accurately characterized by the word "equality" (too
easily supplanted by identicalness), but rather a triad condition of *self-
determination, autonomy,* and *sufficiency.*

Do not mistake the position that sufficiency is the ideal goal as an Uncle
Tomism for an administrative position that an old basketball and a three-
game season are "sufficient" for the woman's team. Women legally must be
granted access to appropriate proportions of public funds and facilities
based on ratios of student population and the like. Whether to utilize
immediately the entire total of this sum? When to utilize it? How to utilize
it? These are the questions of self-determination, autonomy, and sufficiency
which must be left to women sport administrators, coaches, participants.

Resisting the passive acceptance of a pre-existing athletic administrative structure calls for the provision for dynamic change processes in girls' and women's athletic programs. Further, these change processes must be attuned to an ever-evolving idea of *what women want* in their collegiate athletic programs and what steps must be taken to bring wishes to reality. Futurists like Alvin Toffler caution women not to imagine that next month, next year, or in five years they will "have our problem solved," "have the program we want," "have the crisis period over." Such is not to be. Change is the only certainty; and either direct it or submit helplessly to it. To paraphase Daniel Bell in *Daedalus The Year 2000*, we must make efforts now to identify the future consequences of present decisions, to anticipate future problems, to design alternative solutions so that our sport society has options and can make moral choices rather than be constrained to one choice as is often the case when problems descend upon us unnoticed and demand an immediate response.

To sum, college and university administrators can best serve the development of athletic programs for women by: assuring (beginning yesterday) that equitable funding, personnel and facilities are available to women; and assisting and encouraging the women responsible for the women's athletic program to develop a process for sport administration which is attuned to evolving philosophical direction, and systematic identification of the steps necessary to bring the *real* program closer to the *ideal* direction.

Within this process-oriented sport administration, certain thorny issues will seemingly defy resolution in the next few years. Some of these tend to be issues revolving around "women's athletics" as *athletics* and some revolve around "women's athletics" as *women's programs*. Space considerations make the detailed analysis of these issues impractical, but some should be briefly explored.

A key consideration in women's collegiate athletics as a sub-set of all athletics is the promulgation of more humanistic connotations of sport and athletics. The search for humanistic athletics has an important priority — the development of organizational structures within collegiate sport which foster sensitivity to student needs and interest rather than static perpetuation of the status quo and, coincidentally, themselves.

This is a time of sport establishment under fire. Whether one speaks of IOC, USOC, AAU, NCAA, AIAW or whatever, the amount of criticism leveled is intense and widespread. Much of the criticism is justified, and a great deal of it centers around the exploitation and impotence of the sport performer.

Within women's collegiate athletics, it is to be hoped that the co-operative governance efforts of administrators, coaches, officials, and participants could be maintained and increased. At the same time, it appears that some women collegiate performers want their athletics "laid out and waiting for them" like the clothes their mothers used to provide. Olympians are bitterly decrying that athletes have no control over the sport experience which should be theirs. Oh, yes, women sport performers need so much more provided for them in their athletics, but they must avoid becoming consumers of their sport. Historically, the DGWS has emphasized the need for faculty-student guidance groups to direct women's sport. These groups, which do exist in virtually all schools, should grow and never disappear under the assumption that a student performer's time in sport is *always* best spent on the practice field.

With student needs uppermost, sport administrators might also utilize this time of upheaval in sport organization to rethink and reanalyze the administrative placement of athletics within the setting of higher education. What are the implications of considering athletics in each of the following?

1. As a laboratory for integrated learning, properly belonging under a department of physical education.
2. As a recreation program for a highly skilled minority residing in the student services or campus recreation area.
3. As an honors program in movement arts with credit for participation analogous to an independent study opportunity.
4. As an applied arts or professional-vocational program leading to a professional career in athletics.

A greater sensitivity to student needs and interests is surely one aspect of promulgating humanistic athletics.

Another aspect which should occupy some effort is the redefinition of sport and athletics as a form of mutual self-development rather than symbolic warfare. Sport-as-battle is very familiar in forms as diverse as the terminologies and slang of sport (witness "killing" one's opponent, "smashing" the bird or ball, "wiping out" an opponent, and the like) and forms including the very form of sport itself. As examples, note the number of sports built around a theme of protecting one's home base or territory from incursion and, conversely, attempting to violate or take the opponent's space. For many reasons, sport-as-battle has a pervasive connotation of masculinity and exists as a domain into which women have tried most uncomfortably. And yet the agonistic ideal of Greek athletics (the well-spring of so much of Western sport) was rooted in the concept that only through the magnificence of one's opponents' struggle could winning provide ultimate meaning. Such a conception of sport cannot be dismissed as an idealistic absurdity. Such a struggle was experienced in a southwest regional A.S.A. championship in 1964. Team A entered the finals with one loss and one pitcher while its opponents had zero losses and two pitchers. Team A won the first game 2-1 in 7 innings, and its same pitcher proceeded through 28 scoreless innings more in the second game. Each team had a few opportunities to score but flawless play continued the shutouts. Each pitcher had over 35 strikeouts in the 29 innings. Finally, in the bottom of the 29th inning (36th for most), a twist of fate decided the game. In such a contest, as tired legs pump on, as hook-slide scratched knees and thighs bleed, as pitching arms become heavy, the adversary (as so well-expressed by Olga Connally) becomes not the opponent but rather fatigue, muscular weakness, mental lapse. Above all, one desires to see the game positively won, not forfeited by poor play. This orientation toward sport is not sheer idealism; certainly it is not sexist. It is humanistic. In a world where people can no longer do battle with each other and survive, it is a way of sport and athletics to joyously adopt and promulgate through college sport.

What of women's athletics as women's programs? The AIAW, in its structure and function in the commitment seen of its officers, is devoted to dramatically increasing the athletic and other movement-oriented programs for women as a part of the total diversification of life-style opportunities for females. Many women may not accept that this is so. The divisive effects of the controversy over athletic scholarships have placed AIAW often in an adversary position vis-a-vis women's political groups, numbers of students, some of the brightest most able women in the field. One may support the policies against athletic scholarships for women and yet be heartsick over the misunderstandings of interests and purposes which the policies fanned.

At present, these restrictions have been removed, but there is still great concern over the place of women's athletics in the women's movement. To the degree that women demand the barring of men from their programs, they are invoking a hybrid of special, protective legislation. When the law-suits came tumbling upon the various men's athletic organizations, suits in which women were demanding to be allowed on the one school athletic team (the men's team), these organizations might have made a stand themselves for separate men's and women's teams. For whatever reasons, noble or not, they simply sidestepped (by technically removing the restrictions barring women) and left to AIAW the task of proving the case for special treatment.

Another area in which the AIAW-DGWS position would evoke misunderstandings and disagreements with feminist philosophy is in the insistance on the priority of placing women in roles of coaches, trainers and officials in athletics rather than supporting the currently fashionable line of advocating "the most qualified person" for such positions. The "most qualified person" line is almost a surefire applause-getter and, frankly it could be regarded as what sports announcers would call a cheap shot. It is incredibly difficult to prove that a woman is the "most qualified person" to committees that make national and international selections of coaches and officials. Facetiously, it would be far easier for a woman to be elected President of the United States than selected Executive Director of NCAA. To specify that a woman will be the coach of a particular international team is undemocratic and probably illegal, but (for right now, at this point in time) it should be attempted whenever possible if it is necessary to help a qualified woman into a position she would not otherwise attain.

In conclusion, one of the most pervasive effects of the Equal Rights Amendment will be to affirm the absolutely complementary nature of the male/female relationship within society. Every change in women's role in society has a necessary effect, intended or not, on men's roles. As women's athletics change, men's athletics must be altered inevitably in ways that may not be anticipated. The legal courts are now supporting women's claims that the playing fields and funds so long denied must be shared equitably. Many men athletics, coaches, and administrators will feel nothing if not indignation at the sharing process which will now evolve. Women athletics, coaches, administrators will feel the pains as well because of merged destinies. Furthermore, women's success as a minority group winning its time on the diamond will encourage other "minority groups" to strike for their time in the sun. By this is meant minority groups like men's rugby, crew, cross country, skiing, co-educational activities, intramurals, and sport clubs.

Liberation and change, these are the energies that light women's lives as surely as the atomic explosion did a generation ago. It is fervently hoped that society is granted the wisdom to use *this* energy wisely.

Reflective Thoughts

Anita Aldrich

ANITA ALDRICH, Chairman of the Department of
Physical Education for Women at Indiana University,
Bloomington, is a Past President of the American
Association for Health, Physical Education, and
Recreation.

Reflecting on the past few years in women's sports identifies the following points as being meaningful:

1. There has been a lack of research regarding women in athletics during a time when competition has been increasing rapidly.
2. Up until the past eight or ten years, there has been continual emphasis on women in the home and the role of motherhood. Unfounded concern for women in competition appeared repeatedly in the literature. Research was sparse concerning the effects on women involved in high level competition.
3. Depression years were not conducive to expanding educational programs. Increased finances to instigate or continue athletics for women were not included in school or college budgets.
4. Rural populations surrounding small school organizational units did initiate girls' basketball and volleyball. Basketball was especially popular. The coaching was not always scientifically founded, but games were well attended, and there was much enthusiasm. The girls' teams became unifying components of communities.
5. It is possible girls and women's sports were not outstanding because women educators were reluctant to assume added responsibilities of coaching, travelling with a team, and officiating.

It would be well to consider these points of significance.

School administrators, deans, college presidents, women physical educators, and coaches have been reluctant to refer to competition for women as interscholastic or intercollegiate athletics. The program has been referred to as "extramural." Sports Days and Play Day experiences are different from the competition in which girls and women participate today. To name high-level competition for women was a bold step.

A strong point must be accorded the procedure required of an institution seeking membership in AIAW. It was an excellent requirement that made it necessary for a chancellor or president and the dean to sign the form requesting membership. The requirement both disseminated information on the purpose of the Association as well as committed the institution to the acceptance of the policies and procedures of the Association.

Professional women have been forced to establish policies and procedures for organizing and administering athletes.

Emphasis on a new dimension of achievement by women has received time, attention, and publicity. Many girls and women have enhanced their self-images through high-level competition.

And now to project matters of concern for the future.

1. What are to be the relationships of collegiate programs to public school programs?

2. Will women, as well as men, who have been competitors become coaches? Many men who have competed, then coached, have become administrators (principals, superintendents). What were their experiences as athletes that allowed them to become successful administrators? Women should take note; self-discipline, training, winning, losing when it really hurts, team effort, specialization within the game — all of these factors may be pertinent.

3. Women outside the major program are competing in athletics. They will also wish to coach and officiate.

4. Surely common rules for play will evolve. Cannot research lead to one set of rules which will be interchangeable in U.S. public schools and colleges as well as internationally?

5. Women must learn to coach girls and women.

6. There will be a need for women trainers.

7. The women's athletic program should not be a carbon copy of the men's program. (Have you noted woman players, as they are introduced preceeding a game, running out on the floor and striking the fingertips of the other players?)

8. Decisions must be made regarding mounting pressures for recruiting and scholarships either within or without the stated policies of AIAW.

9. Within cutbacks and stringent budgets, administrators are going to find it difficult to employ or designate faculty to administer women's athletic programs. Salaries or stipends for coaches of individual sports and team sports will be difficult to obtain.

10. Administrative leadership within athletic departments in both interscholastic and intercollegiate programs will become increasingly important. Women must be educated in the conduct of athletic affairs.

11. The use of facilities will increase, and equitable use of facilities must be arranged.

12. Superintendents, deans, athletic directors must be kept abreast of the development and direction competition for women is taking. These programs must be educationally sound and, consequently, they must progress through the proper organizational channels.
13. Men and women, knowledgeable in high-level competition, should contribute to the expansion of involvement of the U.S. State Department in athletics abroad.
14. Increased competition for women will, no doubt, lead to increased Olympic participation on the part of athletics, coaches, officials, trainers, and other related personnel. Professional recommendations that the government consider organization and finances to enhance the cultural benefits of athletics to this nation and its constituency are in order.

It will be through the concerted efforts of teachers, coaches, administrators, and fine women athletes that the program will continue to grow. The quality of the programs should enhance the lives of the participants, and society should benefit from girls and women in sports.

The
Olympic
Games

Past Olympic Reflections

Nell C. Jackson

NELL C. JACKSON, from the University of Illinois,
was the Head Coach of the 1972 United States
Women's Olympic Track and Field Team. She has been
an Olympic track competitor, a teacher, a professor,
and a coach.

The 20th Olympic Games will go down in history as the Game of "buts."

"The competition was great but—."

"The facilities were fantastic but—."

"The village was convenient and well equipped but—."

"The food was plentiful but—."

"The athletics were friendly but—."

"The village was secure but—."

And they'll go on and on and on.

Numerous changes and innovating ideas were apparent in Munich. In the old days, officials timed how fast sprinters ran, how far the discus was thrown, and the moment that swimmers touched the finish line stopwatches were "clicked." All of that was changed in the 20th Olympic Games. The stopwatches and tape measures have gone, the cameras and prismatic reflectors have arrived. Human error will probably not be a factor in sports like track and field and swimming in the future. The time it took a person to push the stopwatch compared to the quicker reaction of a camera might just have been the difference between a world record and another good race in Munich. Finish places in all running races were determined by the camera (electronic equipment). In the sprint races, photographs were available seconds after the finish of the race indicating not only the order of finish, but also the official time for each person. In the longer races on the track, a film up to 130-feet long was available. The developing process was so quick that this film could be projected on a 3x3 foot screen within 60 seconds of the finish of the race, with the results accurate to .003 of a second. The photo-timing operation was so well planned that an alternate plan was operative if one runner blocked out another runner, or if the camera failed.

False starts? The starting blocks in each lane were electronically connected to the starter's gun. When a runner left the starting block too soon, the gun would not fire.

In the field events, electronic measuring devices developed by Zeiss, similar to those used in surveying, replaced the tape measures. When a discus or javelin landed, an invisible measuring beam was sent out by an

73

instrument in a cabin above the viewing stands and reflected in a prism to measure the distance. Measurements were reported on the huge electronic scoreboards at either end of the stadium and also at the location of each field event almost instantaneously.

In swimming events, timing was handled by an electronic touch system in each lane at both ends of the pool.

Overall, the scoreboard data at Munich was capable of being changed 12 times a second with a transmission system supposedly 220 times faster than that used at the 1968 Olympics.

In spite of all of these fantastic improvements in some sports, the 1972 Olympic Games, unfortunately, will not be remembered for its stirring moments and scenes of surprise or success in the athletic arenas. Instead, the tragedy of criminal terror and innocent death will always cloud the memory as one attempts to focus his vision on the sporting accomplishments of the athletes from around the world. Even if one does remember some of the stirring moments, the ironies of what happened to some of our fine competitors such as Rick DeMont, Eddie Hart, Rey Robinson, Jim Ryun and the U.S. basketball team will slant his view forever.

The Rhodesian admission controversy, the pole vault decision, the banishment of Matthews and Collett by the IOC, will be recalled quicker than those moments of competition that deserve our respect.

Worthy to be remembered were the winning performances by talented people who earned the right to stand taller, for a moment, than others as dedicated and as talented.

No excuses can be made for the lack of success of the United States in women's track and field. A comparison of performances at Munich with the performances in the Olympic trials indicated, for the most part, the girls performed up to their potential at that time. Except for a few instances, U.S. girls are not at this time in the same class as the Eastern European girls who captured most of the medals.

Renate Stecher, of East Germany, became the first winner of the Olympic sprints, 100 and 200 m., since Wilma Rudolph. Renate accomplished her goal with finality, leaving no doubt that there was anyone in the world equal to her on the running track.

Two other exceptional athletes also proved themselves during the course of the competition: Hildegard Falck, W. Germany, ran the 800 m. in 1:58.6 (in fact, all places in that event were 2:00.0 and better); Ludmila Bragina, USSR, 1,500 m., 4:01.4, a new world's record.

On the running track, the outstanding U.S. athlete was Kathy Hammond who won the bronze medal in the 400 and anchored the 4 x 400 m. relay and Iris Davis who placed 4th in the 100 m. Kathy kept secure the second place standing of the U.S. In the field events, Kathy Schmidt placed third in the javelin giving the U.S. its first medal in that event for quite some time.

Where does the U.S. team go from here? Munich should have taught a great deal. Support and change must be provided by the International Olympic Committee (IOC), International Sports Federations, and National Olympic Committees for improvement in the future.

One of the greatest dangers facing the Olympic Games is "gigantism." The program is growing. Two sports were added in Munich, archery and team handball. Canoeing for women will be added in Montreal. The number of participating countries is increasing (61 countries in women's track and field). There are technical complications in the tendency of all the international sports federations to diminish their responsibilities and then to continually increase the number of events in their sport.

Bringing it closer to home, the U.S. Olympic Team is in danger of losing its international prominence. The U.S. Olympic Committee is going to have to reallocate its priorities if its sports programs expect to keep in step with some of the European countries.

The Women's Track and Field Program needs a financial shot in the arm. More qualified coaches are needed to work with young people; it would be desirable to have the physiologists, doctors in sports medicine, biomechanist and the coaches work together as a team in the U.S.

U.S. sports programs can no longer allow social permissiveness to have the kind of influence that has been seen over the past four years.

The Olympic Games will continue, and U.S. girls will continue to participate. The only question that arises at this time is: How serious will U.S. attempts be next time?

Looking Forward to Montreal

Olga Connolly

OLGA CONNOLLY, from Loyola-Marymount
University in Los Angeles, five times an Olympic
competitor, was elected by her fellow athletes (both
male and female) to carry the United States flag in the
1972 Olympics at Munich.

The pilgrimage to Montreal, if it is to be worth the investment of time,
hope, and money, has to travel beyond the limits of a highway cut through
the desert and marked with one-directional arrows. A maze of pathways
have to be climbed, all of which, in their delicate conquest of obstacles,
will eventually meet at the top of a mountain. Some of the paths, as has
been done in the past, will be trod by loners — the young men and women
and their coaches, whose desire, perseverance, and good fortune will fulfill
their ambitions to represent the United States in the Olympics. Other
pathways will have to be mapped and cut through the wilderness by the
leaders in the fields of sport and physical education.

At this point little is known about what kind of future leadership can
be expected from the U.S. Olympic Committee. In the past, that
organization largely neglected its responsibility for the development of
Olympic sports in the U.S., and literally abdicated its responsibility to
enable self-made champions to reach their utmost potential. That is why
the rest of the world has caught up with, and is surpassing the U.S. in the
majority of Olympic sports. But, with the outcry of criticism from veteran
athletes, coaches, local officials, the general public, and some Congressmen
and Senators, a variety of changes in the organization of amateur sports
has been recommended.*

There is no doubt that enthusiastic, broad-minded, national leadership
is needed in the field of sports. Such a body's zeal, capacity for an unbiased
assessment of needs and problems, and innovative, head-on confrontation
with old grievances would inject sunlight and energy into the veins of the
sports system. But even if that inspiring leadership is lacking, it does not
mean that individuals should sit back and wait for the miracle.

In a democratic society, everyone is important. Everyone carries a
responsibility. In a country as large as the U.S., the value of a grass-root
initiative can, and at times must, surpass the value of the initiative from

---

* Following Olga Connolly's criticism of the U.S. Olympic Committee, 1972 *Olympic
Book,* which all the athletes receive as a souvenir, did not mention her as the captain of
the team and the flag bearer. The book also omitted mention of the women's
discus event.

the top. But, before such initiative can be exerted, some kind of philosophy towards the Olympic movement needs to be set, and then priorities established based on that philosophy.

The question asked most often since Munich is, "Are the Games worth preserving?" There are a couple of answers to this question. The very least the Olympic Games do is to strengthen the position of the international sports federations and to act as a means of communication among nations. The Olympic movement is based upon the acceptance of national representation from countries all over the globe. The smallest units are encouraged to come and compete alongside the large powers. Indeed, the Olympic arena serves as a good equalizer. Where the small countries have no way of competing with the large nations in technological advancement or in a sophisticated war potential, they can prove in the context of the Olympic Games that their peoples have as much determination, stamina, and physical and spiritual endowment as anyone. And that's an important message. If understood in all that it implies, it is a reason valid enough for even a severe critic of the Olympic movement to acknowledge that the Games are worth preserving.

Some who are concerned with the mounting misery of mankind and with the resources that could be used to forestall it, but which are being misdirected into the means of destruction, would naturally like to hear the leaders of the Olympic movement proclaim that the communication in the Olympics must go beyond the boundaries of a sporting clash. They would like to see the Olympic leaders commit themselves openly to the cause of peace. After all, mankind needs peace as much as it needs air, bread and water. Unfortunately, the leaders of the International Olympic movement have not yet reached that degree of intellectual sensitivity.

Munich evidenced over and over again that the sincere and mankind-oriented individual moves towards the furtherance of peace have been crudely misinterpreted for some sort of political activism of special interest groups. While the seed of an effective work towards international brotherhood can never be smothered in the Olympics, the question remains whether it ever shall bloom and bear visible fruit, or whether it shall remain lying dormant in the general atmosphere of the Olympic conquest.

It is assumed that the Olympic Games are primarily a battleground for the scientifically, professionally-trained superathletes from every corner of the world. There are no amateurs competing in the Olympics anymore.

It is a class of superathlete, professionally and, mainly, scientifically trained in methods that haven't been dreamed of in the U.S. The Olympics should be treated as the answer to man's belligerency that has developed throughout the history of his struggle for survival. Bloody wars, no matter how technologically advanced, are barbaric. The Olympic conquest is then an ideal, civilized war. It is a war worth supporting. The victory in the Olympic competition brings slavery to no one, and the defeat does not shatter the mutual respect of the adversaries. The victory rewards the dedication of an individual to perfecting his or her sports prowess or type of art expression (for expression through sports may be considered as another form of artistic expression). For the nation represented, it brings honor untainted with cruelty and an honor which serves as an inspiration to its youth.

This, then, arrives at the obvious goals of nations who want to derive the greatest benefits from their participation in the Olympic Games. They must utilize the enthusiasm generated by their participation in the Olympics for strengthening their people's enjoyment of physical activities. And the nations have to give special care and appreciation to their champion athletes or they will not be able to withstand the pace of the other countries.

In the U.S., the task of meeting these challenges is a complicated one. If met successfully, nevertheless, it would ensure a really invigorated new future of the nation.

Perhaps more than anything else, this task requires an education of the public towards understanding and appreciation of amateur sports. Without such education millions of young people will continue to be confronted with only a woefully meager choice of physical challenges. The schools, and the recreation leaders especially, have to perform a mammoth job of counteracting the pressures of professional sports promoters and introducing the American youth to the excitement, spiritual exhilaration, and tremendous sense of accomplishment offered by all sports. It means, of course, that the scale of values must first be reexamined. Can it be seen that a young wrestler deserves to get as much help and as much credit as a young football player? Can it be seen that a high-school girl volleyball player has to be given as much opportunity to develop her skills as a high-school boy basketball player? Unless these are seen, nothing can be done for the Olympic movement in this country.

At the end of each day, perhaps, every physical educator and recreation leader should ask himself or herself two questions: What have I done today towards the physical development of every youth I'm responsible for? What have I done today towards the development of Olympic sports in my country? The work begins with every physical education and recreation leader. They cannot keep sitting still; they might be sitting still for 50 years.

In regard to sitting still, consider the California State elementary school textbooks, *The Basic Goals in Spelling*. Spelling books for grades four, five, and six, transitional in their format to regular textbooks, are divided into 35 units each. Nearly each unit is introduced by a major, almost page-long, colorful illustration of some activity. They show truck driving, travel by a jet plane, research work in a laboratory, the use of a telescope, different kinds of ball games, canoeing, archery, and so on. Every one of those illustrations, 35 in each of the three texts, features a boy or a man. This is shocking. Girls and women are pictured only in small sketches within the text, and they are shown sitting, standing, singing, hanging the laundry, taking dictation, or sweeping. In another, similarly biased text, is a picture of a standing girl, accompanied by a rhyme that read something like:

> Ellen at the hill top,
> Ellen at the hill,
> Ellen at the hill top hill,
> Standing still, still, still.

In the fields of physical education and sports Ellen has been standing still for altogether too long. On her path to Montreal, Ellen needs meaningful encouragement, opportunity, and appreciative interest in her competition.

Back in 1949, when the Soviet Union decided to enter the Olympic Games for the first time, they knew how hard it would be to excel among the traditional Olympic powers, so they concentrated on training their women. At the 1952 Olympic Games in Helsinki, the Soviet women swept away so many gold medals that the Soviet Union became the winner of the unofficial, but sought-after-by-everybody, total medal count. It was the Soviet *women* who won it.

To claim that the American woman is a specimen that differs in her potential from her Soviet counterpart is a detrimental fallacy as well as an offense. To believe that one has to be physically weak in order to be beautiful is equal nonsense. To say that the American girl is not interested in physical challenge is a generalization that can be disproved by taking note of girls' physical expressiveness at the elementary school level where they run and enjoy themselves. By the junior high-school age, unfortunately, the girls are so intimidated by the social prejudices of their elders that, in the effort to appear "feminine," they start suppressing their natural desires to run, jump, shout, and play. It's the age where they start smoking, too.

There is one male coach, author of a book on basketball, published only a couple of years ago, who makes offensive remarks about women. He considers himself a really great basketball coach. He is on a "masculine trip." He uses a drill in which he asks seven boys to form a circle, then takes six towels and throws them into the circle. He makes the boys fight for the towels. Naturally one of the boys ends up without a towel, and that, in the eyes of the coach, qualifies him as a coward. The author has another drill, which he calls the "Pink Panty" drill in which the boy who loses is forced to wear ladies' pink underwear for the whole day until the next practice. The team addresses the player as "Miss." Society must ride right over such people and combat such prejudice.*

The only way to fight this type of social prejudice is to bring up girls and women with high standards of physical education. People reveal prejudice without realizing it. If an eight- or nine-year old boy dribbles a ball incorrectly, he might be told, "Come on, buddy, this won't get you anywhere; this is how to dribble." But if a girl dribbles somewhat awkwardly, the comment would be, "She's good for a girl."

Excellence has to be demanded from both boys and girls at any level, as well as improvement of their performances with increasing age. And then girls must have the equal opportunity to excel in sports. Indeed, both of these are musts. This should not be a nation that's 50% physically fit, it must be 100% physically fit! This, then, is the second task to undertake on the road to the next Olympic Games.

There is a third, equally important road to travel before this nation can knock confidently at the Olympic gate in Montreal. Decent recreational facilities must be built in every American ghetto.

One of this nation's most populated, impoverished, and illiterate areas is the San Francisco Chinatown. The life in that ghetto may be filled with lost dreams, but it is far from a being dreamy site. There is no decent recreational facility in the San Francisco Chinatown.

---

* The writer's dream is to put on pink panties and challenge this man to play her one-on-one basketball. (She was a member of the Czechoslovakian National Basketball team prior to her track and field participation.)

In Los Angeles, there is the Pico-Union area where some 30,000 people are choking every summer in the smog with no open space to which to escape. Until fairly recently, they did not have a single spot where a mother could take her tot to play on the swings or a slide. It took years of struggle, applications for aid, rejections and labor of volunteers before they converted a small dust bowl near the freeway into what's called a pocket playground. If you'd drive by it, you'd probably hardly notice it. But the tiny playground is there, a tear of love amidst the decay of the inner city.

The U.S. must create open spaces, bring fresh air, and offer outstretched arms to those brother and sister Americans who have never enjoyed the recreational privileges that have been available to suburbanites.

These are the foundations on which to build a meaningful Olympic program in this country. Teams that will be bred on such foundations cannot fail to add enlightenment to the Olympics, and will bring home prestige and glory. They will be the wished-for, motivated teams. And if this nation will scale the heights of Olympia along these paths, there will be no other country on earth which would deserve the Olympic prestige and glory more than the United States of America.

Women
In
Athletics

The Masculine Obsession in Sports

Jack Scott

JACK SCOTT is chairman of the Department of
Physical Education and Director of Athletics at Oberlin
College. He was Director of the Institute for the Study
of Sport and Society and is the author of *The
Athletic Revolution*.

On one airplane flight from Cleveland to Minneapolis, there were fifty-two male passengers, two female passengers, and two or three men up front flying the plane. There were about four or five additional women on the plane serving almost all the men who were on the plane. The men were in charge; the men were the pilots and the copilots. Most of the men on the plane, according to their appearance, were businessmen flying somewhere to conduct important business of the world, helping to keep the world running. Except for two passengers, all the women on the plane were stewardesses. They were smiling, pampering the men. They were dressed as the men who run the airlines tell them how to dress to appear attractive to the men on the plane. Unfortunately that little microcosmic world that existed on that flight from Cleveland to Minneapolis all too well represents not only the American athletic world, but American society in general.

The social order that existed on that airplane did not come about by accident. In fact, it was no more of an accident than the fact that the people who were selected to serve as guides at the 1973 AAHPER national convention all happened to be quite attractive, young teenage women dressed in miniskirts. The stag party atmosphere of American athletics, unfortunately and quite sadly, also was brought right home to the national convention. The various forms of play, sport and athletics that exist in this society are some of the primary forces of socialization that are helping to perpetuate the kind of microcosmic world that existed on that airplane and that, once again, exists throughout all levels of society.

Arnold Beisser and many other commentators who have looked at sport have pointed out that sport in this society serves as sort of a male masculinity rite. For those who do not already accept this perspective, consider just a few examples.

During a school football game in Scranton, Pennsylvania, the coach sent in a substitute player. The sub had gotten about thirty yards out on the field, running toward his team's huddle, when the coach went from the sidelines and made one of the finest tackles that could be made. He went thirty yards out on the field, tackled the sub, picked him up bodily, carried him back to the sidelines, and never sent him back in that night.

The game was played on a Friday or Saturday evening, and on Monday morning, the team watched the films of the game. All of a sudden that play (the sub being sent in) came up, and the coach kept running it over and over and over. He finally said, "Do you see what he is doing? Look at him, look at him, he is running like a girl." That boy was an embarrassment to the coach.

There is also another famous story about old Knute Rockne, noted for his fiery pep talks that could take any group of young men and turn them into one of the Fighting Irish teams that could manhandle anyone. In one famous game (and this story comes from a sports writer by the name of Paul Gallico) Notre Dame was behind at half time by two or three touchdowns against a team they were supposed to be able to destroy. The team went into the locker room at half-time and sat down very solemnly waiting for Rockne to come into the room and give one of his fiery speeches. About two or three minutes went by, and he didn't show up. Finally, as the tension grew and grew, the referee stuck his head in and said there was only a minute or two to go before the team had to go back out on the field. The team didn't know what had happened to the coach. Finally, Rockne came around the corner, opened the door, the entire team looked up to see who it was, and he said, "Oh, excuse me ladies, I was looking for the Notre Dame football team." Needless to say, Notre Dame won the game.

One other story of even a sadder nature comes from an article by Nathan Hare, a black sociologist writing in *Black Scholar* magazine. He was talking about a fight that many may remember, the one involving Benny Kidd Parett and Emile Griffith in which Parett was killed. Hare writes about the extreme emphasis on masculinity in sports. At the weigh-in ceremony before the bout, Parett called Griffith a "woman" or a "fruit." Apparently he used these terms because Griffith had been a choir boy and is now a designer of ladies' hats. Parett's widow, Lucy, blamed this incident for the bad blood between the fighters and the savage fury of Griffith's punches which killed Parett.

As any male athlete knows, there is nothing worse than being called "feminine" when he makes a mistake in athletics, especially in a contact sport. The coach has one "doomsday" weapon, and he can't use it too frequently or it would lose its effect. All the coach has to do is look at a player, he may not even have to say it, but somehow intimate that the man is "feminine." Actually, the word he would use would be "pussy." And male athletes from twelve-year old kids to thirty-year old professional football players have had tears brought to their eyes by that kind of "condemnation."

84

Quite clearly, when a woman decides to enter the world of sports, there are going to be some problems. In fact, the American athletic world is such a masculine milieu that a recent article about Micki King, one of the finest woman divers in the world, made this point with clarity. In the article, her coach wanted to compliment her, and made the remark that she dives like a man: "That's how I knew she was going to be good, because the very first time I saw her, she dove like a man." How well do men dive? Some have trouble going off the side of a pool. Few really knew how to dive, even if they can go off a board. So quite clearly, what Micki King did was dive correctly; and this was labeled the "masculine way."

What can male athletic directors do about this situation? One of the problems encountered is that some people will suggest that there is really no interest among women students in participating in rigorous, competitive athletics. A number of responses can be made to these people: "If the men's football team had coaches with as little competence as have the coaches available to young women, a college might not have a men's football team." "When there is no athletic program in the first place at a school, quite naturally women who are keenly interested in sports are not going to come to that school. If there weren't a chemistry department, there probably wouldn't be too many students demanding that the school have a chemistry department. Students who are interested in chemistry probably wouldn't go there in the first place."

At most schools, men usually control the athletic facilities. All schools are faced with budget problems, and it is difficult to find more money for anything today. But one thing that can be done without any added expense is to make sure that those facilities are shared fairly between men and women. At times that is going to get some people upset. At Oberlin College, in order to provide adequate locker room space for women in a new $5 million gym that was built only a year ago, the men's faculty locker room had to be abolished. There were some people who got upset about that. At some schools in the country, there have had to be threats to cut off funds for the men's athletic program before the men were willing to share, on an equal basis, the facilities with women's athletic teams.

It is reasonable to say that there should be no increase in men's athletic budgets until women have begun to have the opportunity to have adequate programs. In other words, it is not fair to say each year the men's program will grow by 5% and each year the women's program will grow by 5%. What can be said is that, at this point in time, the men's programs are adequate. Until women students at a particular college or a particular high school have the same general opportunity to participate in athletics that the male students have, there is no justification for increasing the funding for men's athletics.

In this past year at Oberlin College, without any major cutbacks in the men's program (except to allow the men who go on the spring baseball trip to sort of find a place to stay for themselves rather than provide them with ten or fifteen dollars a day), it has been possible to provide all the resources requested by the women's athletic committee. This committee, made up of women faculty and women students, determines the nature of the women's athletic program at Oberlin. In one year, the funding for women's athletics has increased from about $700 to approximately $7,000.

Next year it is going to be another story to find the money. The commitment is that if there is no other alternative, one by one a men's sport will go until there is an equal opportunity for men and women at Oberlin College to participate in intercollegiate athletics. The writer's hope and faith here is that men's athletics means so much to those people who really control most of the major institutions of this society, that all of a sudden from some dark hole they will find money for the women's program in order to save the men's program. It really will be sad if, in an effort to create more problems for those in physical education, the people who have financial power make it the kind of situation where men and women have to fight one another for the scarce resources.

There will probably be an increase in coeducational activity on a recreational level. But meaningful opportunities for women in athletics must include athletic programs for women that basically would be run by women. It is not fair to say, "We already have athletic programs; we will just eliminate the sex distinctions which now exist under which only males can compete, and then we will have equal opportunity." This is one area of American life where equal opportunity means truly "separate but equal." For those who have engaged in a struggle where those words sounded very repugnant, they are hard to say. But, in all honesty, this is one area where that is the reality of the situation.

At the present time when women's athletic programs are very minimal, and there are women at some schools who have a very high level of ability, but who can't find adequate competition in women's programs, qualified women should have the right to participate on their school teams. This is an interim measure for those women whose ability is at such a level that they simply can't find adequate competition in the present women's programs. It is the responsibility of educators to provide them with the opportunity to compete on a high level until such a time as there are adequate women's programs. Oberlin College tried to do that this year, and, unfortunately, was censored by the Ohio Athletic Conference for simply allowing women to swim exhibition status in a dual swim meet.

Behind all this talk about athletic programs for women and athletic programs for men is the concept society holds as to what is masculine and what is feminine. Resistance to the development of competitive athletic programs at times comes from women physical educators just as much as from men physical educators. Hopefully, some day society will begin to talk about not what's "masculine" or not what is "feminine," but what is human.

A year ago I was doing a story on Olga Connolly for *Life* magazine, and I followed her around for a day. I got to her house early in the morning. She has four children she is raising, and like a mother, she did everything that mothers are supposed to do. We left the house after the kids were sent off to school and went to the local YMCA where Olga had permission to use the weight room. She lifted weights because she was training to participate for the fifth time, at age 39, in the 1972 Olympic Games. In order to throw the discus, she had to lift weights. She went into the weight room at the YMCA and she lifted weights the way weights are supposed to be lifted. It is one thing for a woman to go into a weight room and start doing "cute, feminine" kinds of things — the men love it. But it is another thing when a woman goes in there and goes: "Ugh," and lifts weights the way it should be done. Some of the men at the YMCA in Los Angeles actually complained to the director that it was impossible for them to lift weights in the weight room when a woman was in there also lifting weights.

Olga left the weight room at the YMCA and went to Marymount College where she was teaching and counseling. She spent an hour or two counseling students in a very warm and gentle fashion. At noon that day there happened to be a faculty-student basketball game. Olga was the only female faculty member participating in the game. She was up and down the court grabbing rebounds, falling on the floor, knocking people down, getting knocked down herself, but playing basketball basically how basketball is supposed to be played. Does it matter whether she was behaving in a "masculine" way or in a "feminine" way? What did matter was that she was a person who had developed herself so that in any given situation she could behave in a rational, sane way.

In today's society, one should be prepared to behave aggressively, at times, to survive. To have friends, at times one should be prepared to behave in a gentle way. Unfortunately, people are usually atrophied into one extreme or the other. Men know how to be very aggressive and tough, and they often are. Women, on the other hand, usually have been socialized into passivity, and they have that down very well.

The value of women having the opportunity to participate in competitive sport has a social significance far beyond the world of athletics. When people have the freedom to truly choose what form of human movement best suits them — when women on campuses can, for example, feel as free to go into a weight room as they now can to go into a ballet studio, and when a man might decide to leave the football team and take up modern dance and can feel comfortable doing that — then both society as well as the physical education and athletic profession will be much saner. This will happen only when people abandon their obsession with being "masculine" or "feminine," and concern themselves with being human.

The Full Court Press for Women in Athletics

Jan Felshin

JAN FELSHIN is Professor and Director of Graduate Studies at East Stroudsburg State College in Pennsylvania. Jan has written the books, *Perspectives and Principles for Physical Education,* and *More Than Movement: An Introduction to Physical Education.* She has been a provocative thinker in the area of physical education. Her new book, *The American Woman in Sport,* with Pearl Berlin, Ellen Gerber and Waneen Wyrick is due off the press in April, 1974.

The "full court press" is a contemporary female strategy in social and legal frameworks as well as in basketball. It is surprising to find women using pressure tactics. Every female athlete has had to rely on a prevent defense of conciliatory apologetics for the right to participate in the face of aggressive restriction, hostility, and derision. The transition from the limited dribble to the fast break took three-quarters of a century in basketball, and only now is the process of liberation it represents being recognized.

The gallantry of protective attitudes of men toward women has served to idealize feminine ineptitude and undermine aspirations to competence. Both social behavior and sport structures are ritualized assertions of value, and, in our society, both emphasize the initiative and importance of men. The masculine image is admired most as it is actualized in athletic interaction. Contesting, striving, and aggressing provide powerful models for behavior in a domain where status depends upon power, perseverance, daring, and excellence.

The concept of sport as a mirror for masculinity demands its exploitation as a preserve for males. Men seek to maintain the image of women as helpless and subservient to their comfort and needs and the image of sport as a place where the courageous and the mighty prevail.

"Women in sport" has seemed a contradiction in terms, a social anomaly, if you will. The conventional wisdom of what is feminine and what is athletic endorses the stigma of the female athlete and the perpetuation of sport as a masculine assertion. Women have been kept "in their place" in the wonderful world of sport in a variety of ways. They are barred directly from participation in some athletic contests. Whether feminine biology, physiology, psychology, or social role is the rationale, male administrators

---

* Based on a speech delivered at a meeting of the Philosophical and Cultural Foundations Area, AAHPER National Convention, Minneapolis, Minnesota, April 16, 1973.

have simply written the eligibility rules to exclude women. In 776 B.C. in Greece and 1973 A.D. in the United States, men have ordained that, by definition, certain athletics categories exclude women. The mythology of the inability of women to pursue sport is served even when their ability is manifest. The female athlete is labeled an "exceptional" woman, and her femininity challenged or derided. Neither medical evidence nor the athletic participation and success of thousands of women dispels the notion that women engaged in sport are probably abnormal in both their sexual and social predilections. The masculine image of sport is finally protected from women insofar as men's activities are the real and serious ones. In this sense, the unusual involvement requires acknowledgment, as in "girls'" basketball and "women's" softball, and the corollary assumption of these as limited and trivial versions of the "real" thing. Other sports are "feminine" and emphasize grace and beauty when women are involved in them.

The double bind of feminine failure and success avoidance has proved a "tender trap"; the dearth of achievements by women is cited as proof of the inappropriateness of women competing. Women have not dominated many fields, even those traditionally their own. There are not hosts of "great" women artists nor scientists, nor even chefs. When women succeed, success is redefined, and women have accepted the mythic mode and apologized when they transcended its bounds. In sport, women have seemed to accede to their exclusion, exceptionality, and lesser importance. They have assiduously avoided both integration and imitation of men's athletic models, and they have consistently offered assurance that femininity mattered and would be upheld. The pernicious maneuvers that men have used to limit women's programs and enhance their own status and participation have been eagerly endorsed by the victims themselves, and the real issues have been obscured.

There is no need to document the inequality of women in sport. Even *Sports Illustrated* finally did that in a three part series which began on May 28, 1973, with the article, "Sport is Unfair to Women," and the cover banner, "Women are Getting a Raw Deal." In "Part 3: Women in Sport" (June 11, 1973), Bil Gilbert and Nancy Williamson said, "Another far more conservative group, women physical education teachers, is beginning to agitate, if in a very genteel way, for better girls' athletic programs." The point is, of course, that only now is that agitation for the end of sexist practices. The equality revolution of our age has extended to women and to sport. Women in physical education may have been conservative, but consciousness is raised, oppression is obvious, and it is untenable.

Title IX of the Education Amendments of 1972 precludes sex discrimination in athletics. At its Sixth Annual Conference in February, 1973, The National Organization for Women (NOW) passed a resolution stating that it "opposes and actively works to eliminate all forms of discrimination against women and girls in recreation and sport, including school, (college) community physical education, and recreation programs and facilities," and created a Task Force to implement sports policies. Locally, feminist groups have been extremely active and successful. In Reading, Pennsylvania, the local chapter of NOW contacted the school board and immediately obtained increased athletic opportunities for high school girls. Marcia Federbush's brilliant report in January 1973, entitled "Let Them Aspire! A Plea and Proposal for Equality and Opportunity for Males and Females in the Ann Arbor Public Schools," states that the regulations of the Michigan High School Athletic Association that were generally overprotective of girls had been changed to "recommendations" as a result of court cases and the possibility of sexually discriminatory policies.* The Pennsylvania Human Relations Commission report, *Sexism in Education,* contains clear imperatives for the end of sex discrimination in athletics. Court cases in several states have established that per capita expenditures on activities by sex can be an objective measure of discrimination; that girls cannot be prohibited from playing on boys' teams, even in contact sports; that unequal facilities are discriminatory, and so on. And, of course, the Kellmeyer suit against the NEA filed in U. S. District Court for the Southern District of Florida was sufficient impetus for change of the AIAW scholarship policy.

The "second sex," like other socially inferior groups, has had to adopt approval-seeking and humble interpersonal modes. As long as being called "unfeminine" held the terror of social ostracism, women were prohibited from militancy. Women physical educators have always been vulnerable to charges of aggressiveness, and only conciliation with reference to the leftovers of school time, space, and money for their programs has saved them from the vicious attacks presently in evidence. But a raised consciousness about the sources of assumptions about what is "right" for women to do and be has dispelled the terror of attacks on femininity.

Sexism is a social disease, and the time has come to redress the wrongs that are committed because of it. It is too late for the principle of equality alone; women in sport must seek and demand affirmative action on their

---

* The report is available for $2 through Marcia Federbush, 1000 Cedar Ben Drive, Ann Arbor, Michigan 96031.

own behalf through whatever interpersonal and legal means available. This means that *equal* development of programs for men and women is *not* sufficient. The present disequilibrium must be overcome, and the fact that this means cutting programs and expenditures for men and boys must be faced. Executive Order 11246 of the U. S. Department of Health, Education, and Welfare states, "The premise of the affirmative action concept of the Executive Order is that unless positive action is undertaken to overcome the effects of systemic institutional forms of exclusion and discrimination, a benign neutrality in employment practices will tend to perpetuate the *status quo ante* indefinitely." This is obviously true in sport as well as in employment, for sexist assumptions pervade every aspect of athletics. The Supreme Court ruled in May, 1973, that all laws involving classification by sex would be regarded in the future as "inherently suspect." This same attitude is appropriate to all considerations of athletic programs, and the issue of sexism must be confronted in the Little League, the school board, the physical education budget, and the student government.

Legal recourse cannot insure good athletic programs for either men or women, but neither can good programs for girls and women be developed easily within the existing sexist structures of sport. It seems appropriate for women to marshal efforts even at the risk of using "masculine" methods of aggressive and unyielding demand. Whether or not women ultimately will choose to play as members of men's teams or to participate in traditionally men's sports is not the contemporary issue. They must have the right to choose, and courageous women have already challenged the inequities that exist. The feminists in our communities may not be sophisticated about physical education, but they recognize discrimination, and their efforts to broaden opportunities for girls and women in programs must be encouraged. If it is chauvinistic to overprotect women, then it must be avoided by both sexes.

The athletic model designed and perpetrated by men pervades schools and society; and it is, in part, a repellent one. Women cannot, in good conscience, enter a struggle for the prize of brutality, authority, or the exploitation of young athletes. But women have never believed that sport necessitated those things, nor would they foster them in our programs. Men have excluded women from sport because they recognized that it would be changed by them. Let us hope that it will be and that the half of the budget women take will be the half that supported corruption. The issue is the right of women to full participation in a domain that has the potential for the finest human actualization.

The Environmental Effect on the Woman in Athletics

Charlotte West

CHARLOTTE WEST is Professor and Director of
Women's Intramurals and Women's Intercollegiate
Athletics at Southern Illinois University at Carbondale.
She is a past Vice-President of the Midwest Association
for Physical Education of College Women and is very
active in the Division for Girls and Women's Sports.

Very little true knowledge exists about the female athlete. Recent progress
in contributing to a body of knowledge is, however, most encouraging.
There are two approaches to a consideration of the psychological aspects
of the female athlete. One approach would be to attempt to synthesize
recent research findings. In view of both the lack of consensus among the
studies designed to identify personality traits, and the problems in assessing
personality, consideration of the alternate approach appears worthwhile.
This approach would focus on the environment in which the female athlete
finds herself today.

Psychologists readily recognize the importance of the environment in
shaping personality. Strecker defines personality as the psychic endowment
that comes to a person as a result of the interchange between it and the
environment. Allport states that personality is evoked only in relation to
others. Definitions of personality generally imply that personality varies
according to response of an individual to a given situation. Identification of
"given situations" that are typical environments of the female athlete is a
justified approach in light of the close relationship between personality
factors and environmental conditions.

Three rather common environmental conditions exist in which the woman
athlete of today operates and these conditions are termed: "The Lower
Class Citizenry," "The Avocation System," and "The Femininity Diminution
Syndrome." Presumably other conditions exist, but the three selected
conditions are real and exert immeasurable psychological pressures on
women who choose to participate in athletics.

To understand the environmental factors which characterize the first
condition, one must identify and compare the facilities, equipment, and
financial support available in the athletic programs for men in contrast to
the athletic programs for women. This examination and comparison results
in the conclusion that the women are truly not only second-class, but
possibly third-class, or even fourth-class citizens.

93

Faculty members at Southern Illinois University frequently visit area schools as members of a North Central Visitation Team. Several members go on three or four visitations per year so that, through the years, they have visited hundreds of area schools. *At no time* when a school has had two gyms available, have the girls had the privilege of being housed in the newer or the better of the two facilities. This condition is telling the high school athlete something and, obviously, the message for the girls, the second-class citizens, is quite different than the message for the boys, the first-class citizens. In a more typical high-school situation, only one gym is available. Who gets the gym at prime time for an after-school program? — The boys' varsity. And who gets the gym for the prime time when the boys' varsity has an away or a night game? — The boys' junior varsity. The high-school girl who is eager to participate in sports gets still another message. This time, she realizes that she is a third-class citizen.

Frequently a great amount of patience and perseverance is required on the part of the girls simply to get to play. In one instance, a woman physical educator scheduled an after-school volleyball tournament for members of the GAA, knowing that both the boys' varsity basketball team and the JV team would be away. The girls were there, the nets were set up, and the games were about to get underway when the junior-high boys' basketball team appeared. They had come over to the high school to practice in the large gym. The principal was contacted in order to resolve the problem, since neither group wished to relinquish the gym. Now who got the gym? — The junior-high boys. These girls, now truly fourth-class citizens, once again were denied the opportunity to participate in sports. It is shocking that large numbers of girls continue to be denied the opportunity to participate in sports in situations such as these. Blatant inequities and unfair practices *must* shape the personalities of the people they affect. It takes a true love of sport to counter pressures of this type. It is easier at times just to give up and not participate. It is amazing that more girls have not attempted this mode of escape.

It is also appalling to realize the number of people, men and women alike, who believe that a woman's place in an athletic contest should be relegated to cheering or waving a pom pom. Innumerable instances can be cited which would lend support to the thesis that women athletes belong to a lower-class citizenry. One very recent incident vividly portrays the ignorance and lack of reason which can be displayed by a normally rational person over an emotional issue. (Unfortunately, the question of whether women should participate in varsity athletics remains an emotional issue to some individuals.) One of the women members of the Southern Illinois track and field team went to the University Health Service to take her medical examination. A nurse who was new at the Service gave her a chest X ray since this test was a part of the examination procedure for the male athletes the staff had been examining. Prior to this time, a chest X ray had not been a part of the examination procedure for women athletes. The physical education department became aware of this difference in examination procedures only because a question arose as to who would pay for the chest X ray. The department chairman called the Health Service to see if this phase of the physical exam could be included for all athletes. The chairman stated that if the doctor had determined that this test was important for male athletes, then it must also be important for female athletes. The nurse's response was, "Oh, you mean discrimination? Oh, come on now, you must be kidding!" The nurse literally attempted to shame our chairman for suggesting that the men and women should not be treated differently. One woman colleague in philosophy suggested that since the girls had bigger chests, they may indeed need X rays more than the men!

The second environmental condition in which women athletes operate is termed "The Avocation System." Whereas professional sports for men have served as a vehicle for a rise in social and financial status, a comparable avenue does not exist for women. Successful male athletes can enjoy fame and financial success in a wide repertoire of athletic endeavors, such as baseball, basketball, boxing, football, golf, ice hockey, and tennis to name a few. Women have an extremely limited repertoire. In fact, professional sports for women who seek fame and financial success are limited essentially to golf, tennis and ice skating. The number one winner among the male golfer pockets over $200,000 a year in winnings alone, while the number one winner among female golfers pockets only about $40,000. Contracts and associated benefits are even less lucrative in comparison.

Consider for a moment the professional opportunities available to the female counterparts of three famous college athletes — Bill Walton, Johnny Rogers, Ben Crenshaw. The opportunity for the 6' 5" center on the UCLA Girls Basketball Team would be about "zip." The opportunity for the left halfback on the Nebraska Girls Field Hockey Team would be less than zip. And the opportunity for the number one girl golfer at the University of Texas would be only about zip plus. Without the attractive financial offers available in professional sports, what percentage of the now-famous male athletes would have endured the long hours and the hard work solely for the love of playing? The counter arguments about the undesirable nature of external incentives have been used effectively to perpetuate the avocation system.

These comparisons do not constitute an attempt to make a value judgment about the virtues of professional sports for women, but rather suggest that the personality development of participants may be very different when the sport is an avocation in lieu of a vocation. Engagement in professional sports undoubtedly strongly affects the personality of the participant.

The condition which presents the greatest psychological dilemma for women athletes is called "The Femininity Diminution Syndrome." The notion that participation in vigorous competitive athletics makes a woman less of a woman, that is, less feminine, pervades the thinking of a large portion of our society. Absolutely no scientific evidence exists to support such a notion, but the idea does persist. This misconception manifests itself in many ways. Suppose that several attractive women are selected as subjects for a study in which they participate in a variety of athletic events. Assume that each event is performed with a high level of skill. (Some people may find this assumption is not too tenable, convinced that pretty girls are not well-skilled and conversely, that well-skilled girls are not very pretty.) Subsequently, each subject is to be rated on a scale which represents degree of femininity. Would the discus thrower, straining to attain maximum force, receive the same score as the figure skater executing a scale? Would the softball player, sliding into third base, receive the same score as the gymnast executing a tinsica? Most viewers would rate the figure skater and the gymnast significantly higher on the femininity scale, although the subject might be the *same person* in both cases. Girls who enjoy playing basketball, soccer and field hockey have wrestled with this dilemma. Much less pressure exists for girls who enjoy swimming, golf, and tennis since these activities are not considered as "threatening" with respect to a girl's femininity. A girl who loves to run, to hurdle, to throw has to accept the fact that many people, often the one or ones about whom she cares the most, will consider her less feminine which, of course, means the same thing as more masculine, although "less feminine" has a more acceptable connotation. Several outstanding women athletes have been in the torturous position of having to give up participation in sports because of a disapproving husband. It is a pleasure to coach a girl whose husband understands and respects the joy that she obtains in participating in sports. And it is a displeasure to coach the confused girl whose husband does not understand and does not respect his wife's desire to be an athlete. A dual standard exists for male and female athletes. How many male athletes have given up participation in collegiate sports because of disapproving wives? Why can't a husband be as proud of his wife's athletic prowess as a wife normally is of his?

Adjustments to inferences about diminished femininity are perhaps the most difficult the female athlete has to make. Solutions to the problems are most difficult. The greatest boon to women's sports in this sex-oriented society could be the widespread distribution of the findings that frequent participation in vigorous physical activity is the answer to the previously elusive and long sought after aphrodisiac. There would certainly be as much truth to the premise that participaion in competition athletics is the panacea for frigid women as to the premise that participation in competitive athletics makes a woman masculine.

If, indeed, the personality of an individual is dependent upon the environment, then the determination of personality traits of persons with a common environment appears to have merit. Three common environmental conditions which have undoubtedly influenced the personalities of female athletes have been identified. "Lower Class Citizenry" has been quietly accepted by women for decades, and women as amateurs in the sports world is the norm. "The Femininity Diminution Syndrome" is an obstacle against which women have learned to defend themselves. These environmental conditions are beginning to change since it has now become evident that the hand that rocks the cradle can also rock the boat!

Hundreds of years of contention with these psychological barriers have toughened the will of the woman in athletics. Once these barriers are broken, as they seem now to be with the help of the federal government which has a way of Christianizing deterrents to the counter-culture, concurrent change will appear in the psychological character of the female athlete. For most women in athletics, the change cannot come too soon.

Welfare
of Women
in Sports

Anxiety Levels Experienced by Women in Competition

Mary Roland Griffin

MARY ROLAND GRIFFIN, from Winthrop College
in Rock Hill, South Carolina, relates some recent findings
of importance to women coaches.

In 1965 the first Institute on girls' and women's sports was held. This
represented an initial step by women physical educators toward recognition
of resurgence of interest in highly competitive sports for women. Among
the purposes of this institute was "To encourage and provide information
for leadership to administer competition for girls and women." Great strides
have been made in these eight short years. . . . DGWS appointed a
commission on Intercollegiates for Women in 1965, and the committee
published guidelines in 1969, followed by the formation of AIAW and now
the coaching interest area. Leadership must still be provided for
administering the competition for girls and women . . . as evidenced by
the most recent guidelines for talent scholarships in athletics for women.

As women get into coaching, they are becoming more and more aware of
the psychological aspects of sports and competition. It is natural that
resurgence of interest in competition should bring about research in this
area. The number of conferences and institutes on women and sport in the
summer of 1973 indicates a desire to learn as much as is possible.

The coach wonders about many questions. How does the anxiety level of
a participant vary from one sport to another, from a team sport participant
to an individual sport participant? When does a competitor experience her
greatest level of anxiety? Which players need boosting by pep talks, and
which need calming down? Satisfactory answers to these and other such
questions could prove beneficial to a participant and to a coach.

The topic, "Anxiety Levels Experienced by Women in Athletic
Competition," is rather broad. Its data were derived from research I did
in this area for about a year and half in 1970-71. I became interested in this
for several reasons, having been a secondary school coach, a recreational
league coach and an intercollegiate coach. I began to raise questions: what
types of personalities favored one sport or another? What was the effect of
spectators and parents? What was the effect of the time of day a contest
was played, the reputation of the opponents, and such? Research answered
some of these questions, but may have raised more than it answered.

Some aspects are more demanding physically than others; maybe some
are more demanding psychologically. Some confusion was encountered

99

defining anxiety and its relationship to stress, but finally Cratty's definition of anxiety was accepted: "Sport is a stressor, anxiety is a more narrow term and represents a fear or foreboding." Leaders in physical education are concerned with two fears, fear of failure and fear of harm. Sports anxieties can be traced back to these two.

The next problem was to determine how to measure a person's anxiety. Many of the measures of stress are physiologic, and this would serve; but a more psychological measure was needed, and the best place to get this was to get to the feelings of the person. Taylor's Manifest Anxiety Scale can be used to identify high and low anxious states, but there was need for a more discriminatory scale. Speilberger, a psychologist at Florida State University, has devised a paper and pencil test called the STAI, State-Trait-Anxiety Inventory. He recognizes two types of anxiety within each person. . . . A *trait* anxiety which refers to relatively stable individual differences in anxiety proneness, the tendency to respond to a situation perceived as threatening; and *state* anxiety, which is a transitory emotional condition characterized by feelings of tension and apprehension. This scale provides or describes a continuum, which is good. The scales each consist of 20 statements to which the individual responds: "Not at all, Some, Moderately, Very much."

This instrument was used to find out if differences did exist among age groups and even among sports in what are considered high-level competition.

Three age groups were chosen so that there were definite breaks in the age cycle. The groups were 12 and 13 year olds or the young adolescents, 16 and 17 year olds, the high school age groups, and 19 year old or sophomore level of college and up. Eight sports were selected, four team sports and four individual or dual sports. Basketball, field hockey, softball, and volleyball made up the team sports. Most were played by all age groups in the five southeastern states where the investigator was working, and at least four teams in each of these sports and age groups were used. The four individual sports used were gymnastics, swimming, tennis, and track and field. These, too, were being played by all three age groups. At least 20 participants in each age group of each individual sport made up the sampling. Many were tested, and 682 were used, ranging from 154 in volleyball to 41 in tennis. The youngest tennis group had to be eliminated because it was too small.

100

The STATE Anxiety Scale was administered to all participants as close to the actual contest as feasible, but always within one hour of the competition. In a sense, pre-task anxiety in each of these was measured. The competitive events were selected on the basis of stressful situations such as tournaments. The TRAIT Scales were administered at a later date when no known anxiety or stress was evident.

Scores on STATE Anxiety were analyzed by age groups since this was the primary interest, by sports groups, and by age groups in sports to see if age or sport had a uniform effect over the other. Least Squares Analysis of Variance (ANOV) was used, and the differences in the STATE scores by age groups were significant. The overall mean score on STATE Anxiety was 45.58.

Number Tested	Age	Mean Score
146	12-13	46.84
264	16-17	45.97
272	19+	43.93

The most STATE anxious group was composed of subjects 12 and 13, and the least anxious was the 19+. This may be due to experience in competitive events. The intense competition itself may not diminish, but an individual's ability to handle it may improve with repeated experiences and exposures. Thus, it could be less anxiety producing.

Significant differences in STATE anxiety scores did exist among sports groups.

Gymnastics participants were the most STATE anxious at 50.8, followed by track and field, swimming, tennis, softball, volleyball, basketball and hockey.

Number Tested	Sport	Mean Score
56	Gymnastics	50.8
57	Track and Field	47.8
61	Swimming	46.6
41	Tennis	45.7
86	Softball	44.6
154	Volleyball	44.1
102	Basketball	43.1
125	Field Hockey	41.9

It was interesting that the four individual sports had higher mean scores on State Anxiety than the overall mean and higher than any of the four team sports. This tended to support the hypothesis that women participating in individual or dual sports experience higher levels of anxiety than team sports participants.

It could be that greater pre-task tension and anxiety are characteristic of individual sports, and thus fear of failure would be greater. In the team sports, a poorer than average performance may be masked by skill, cooperation, and team play of teammates. This option is not available to individual sports performers.

The gymnastics participants had the highest STATE Anxiety scores. This could be explained in part by the theories of Vanek and Cratty: "That those activities requiring total body coordination (or where aesthetic purity is the emphasis) engender a great deal of pre-task anxiety." Track and field participants and swimmers also compete against a clock as well as self, and this may add another dimension. The tennis player is dependent upon the play of his opponent to some extent, and this may account for its lower position among the individual sports.

It was interesting to note that the softball players had the highest STATE Anxiety scores among the team sport groups. The performance is dependent on play of teammates and opponents, but as a player becomes a batter, or even a pitcher, this takes on some of the aspects of the individual sport. This could help to explain its position in the ranking.

The interaction ratio was also significant. This showed that the effects of sports or age were not consistent over the other variable on STATE anxiety scores. The change in direction was not always the same. The means of the STATE Anxiety scores for tennis, track and field, softball and volleyball diminished as age increased. Basketball stayed approximately the same for 12- and 16-year olds and dipped slightly in the upper age group. Swimming and gymnastics went up from 12-year olds to 16, then dropped in the 19-year olds but in neither case to as low as the 12-year olds. (See Figure 1.)

TRAIT Anxiety scores were also analyzed and showed significant differences by age and sports groups. This relatively stable quality may have implications as to who chooses which sports. The 16-year olds were the most TRAIT anxious. Peer pressure may be greater here. TRAIT Anxiety means by sports were:

102

Gymnastics	40.26	Overall	38.49
Swimming	39.71	Softball	38.01
Volleyball	39.03	Tennis	37.87
Track and Field	38.57	Hockey	37.86
		Basketball	36.63

Volleyball means shifted into the upper bracket with individual sports, and tennis means were in the bottom group with team sports. It was concluded that TRAIT Anxiety levels of women engaged in competitive sports are significantly different at the chosen three age levels.

The TRAIT Anxiety levels differ among sports, and the effect of age or sport is not consistent over the other variable.

It is known that competition raises anxiety levels, some activities raise it more than others, and, if the level is already at an optimum for a participant, performance may suffer under this added stress. This may help in dealing a little more realistically and with more understanding with the gymnast who appears so high strung, the "super star" who never outgrows the "butterflies," the sub who plays "over her head," or the girl whose practices always outshine her performances in competition. The group pep talks may build up camaraderie or esprit de corps, but do they also build up a performer's anxiety and tension to the feasible stage? Hopefully, this type of research may prove useful to coaches in a wise handling of competitive situations and women participants.

State Anxiety Scores of Women in Three Age Groups and Eight Competitive Sports

Sport	12-13 Years	16-17 Years	19 Years and Up	Direction of Change
Gymnastics	49.11	52.17	51.30	
Swimming	45.74	48.00	46.08	
Tennis	None	47.40	42.85	
Track and Field	51.65	48.18	43.61	
Basketball	43.22	43.56	42.75	
Field Hockey	38.53	42.24	44.34	
Softball	50.71	42.84	40.23	
Volleyball	48.78	43.41	40.28	
			12 16 19	
			13 17 up	

Figure 1

Sociological Aspects of Women in Sports

Betty Menzie

BETTY MENZIE, from Eastern Michigan University, presented this paper at the DGWS National Coaches Conference held at Western Michigan University in September, 1973.

American culture is in a transitional stage in which the place of women is changing and in which women's roles are becoming less well-defined. It is hoped that rapid progress is being made in this direction; a recent observation, however, tends to curb optimism. A busload of children was seen driving into the park during a shower of rain. Within about two minutes, the doors opened, and out rushed about twenty-five fifth-grade boys. They were oblivious of the rain and began to unload boxes of food and carry them to the shelter. After all of the boxes were unloaded, the boys took their fishing rods, baseball equipment and other sporting things and became involved in some active form of entertainment. After about ten more minutes, the doors of the bus opened again, and out came the fifth-grade girls. They were squealing about getting their hair wet, ran to the shelter and sat down. This same scene has probably been enacted in exactly the same way for decades. The boys had learned their roles well, and so had the girls. It was no longer certain that girls' perceptions of themselves were any different today than they were forty years ago.

Sociology is a field that attempts to study and explain human social behavior. The sociologist recognizes that members of a group or of society behave according to rules or standards shared by all, called "social norms." Norms refer to expectations for individuals because of the position in the group they hold or the role they play. Culture itself refers to the total of the ways of behaving, feeling, thinking, learned by man as a member of a particular society. The "proper" way of life is described by norms. To study a culture and determine its style, the sociologist must study all social institutions, organizations, groups, norms and roles in that society. A person's culture shapes his life, and what shapes one's life and influences one is usually valued. Values incorporate the feelings that one has about the basic events in one's life.

How do the people brought up in the culture of the United States view the male? In a study conducted by Broverman and others (1), male and female clinical psychologists were asked to list behavior traits which they felt would characterize the healthy adult female, healthy adult male and the healthy adult ('no sex indicated). The healthy adult male and the healthy adult were characterized as independent, logical, self-confident, and aggressive. The healthy adult female is described as an individual who is dependent, emotional, intuitive and passive. In summarizing this study, Griffin says: "Thus, the findings of Broverman's study suggest that to be both a healthy adult and a healthy adult female is a logical impossibility" (2).

America was founded upon rugged individualism. Men needed to be strong, tough, aggressive and hard if they were to survive. A person with these characteristics was considered manly. Today these attributes are no longer necessary for survival, and there are few places where a man can display his strength, endurance, skill, aggression and toughness. Sport offers this opportunity, and interestingly enough, it is not sufficient to just participate in the sport, it is much more important to win as the final outcome. William Sadler, Jr., a sociologist from Bloomfield College in New Jersey, describes the ideal type coach as:

He endorses a secularized version of the Protestant Ethic, emphasizing the necessity and virtue of hard work, sacrifice, and discipline to achieve mastery, domination, control, and eventually victory. One of his primary values is power. He often demands control over his organization and his athletes; and he hopes to exercise it over his opponents. (5)

Dr. Sadler believes that competition has become a primary value in our culture, has changed from a means to an end, and that athletes have become so important in American life because they reinforce "a competitive work ethic precisely at a time when it is being challenged and tamed in other spheres" (5).

American culture has institutionalized sport. Sport has become a place where a man can test his manliness, where materialism and aggression are rewarded, where skill is a means to achievement. Is it little wonder then that this dependent, emotional, non-intelligent but intuitive and passive, healthy female is not accepted into the realm of sport, an activity which plays such an important part in male expressions of masculinity?

Metheny points out that there are certain forms of sport which are not acceptable for female participation (3). These are wrestling, judo, boxing, weight lifting, hammer throw, the pole vault, the longer foot races, high hurdles and all forms of team games with the exception of volleyball. These are activities which are characterized by bodily contact, application of body force to some heavy object, projection of the body into or through space for long distances, cooperative face-to-face opposition in situations

105

in which some body contact may occur. Most studies indicate that not only men but the majority of women support the view that most sports are within the male domain and that women should not participate in them too frequently, develop much skill, and show much strength. American culture places a high priority upon sport for men, has made sport a social institution, does not place sport in a high priority place for women, and ascribes what could be considered negative behavior traits to the so-called healthy adult woman.

The sociologist looks at language as a form of symbolic communication essential in any culture. All human societies must have some form of communication, and thus man learns a set of symbols and their meanings. Life experiences are expressed through words, and these experiences are shaped by our culture. Language is filled with norms, ways of behaving, and expectations: it involves cultural assumptions and is related to relationships between man and his world and the role which he plays. Language takes the form of words, but also many other forms as well. Non-verbal communication is a timely area of investigation today. Sport terms have become a part of everyday language, which reinforces the idea that sport plays an important role in society. "You aren't following the game plan," it's a "team effort," "quarterbacking" are just a few examples of how language has incorporated sport terms.

Language includes certain expectations, and people respond according to their roles. If a child is continually told that he is very intelligent, a good athlete, good looking, jovial, he will begin to look at himself in those terms. He will be expected to act as though he were intelligent, and he will expect to act as though he were intelligent — unless he is placed into a situation where he is treated otherwise. If this occurs, he may have to change his own perception of himself. What language is used to describe men and women in our culture? Independent, logical, self-confident and aggressive or dependent, emotionally unstable, supporting rather than productive, intuitive rather than intelligent, and passive. What expectations are thus expressed for the male? for the female? If both men and women accept these stereotypes as being the way males and females should be, they will accept them as descriptions of themselves, and they will live up to these expectations. The boys and girls who came off that bus had learned this lesson well. American culture has clearly described the male and female role and has developed words to insure that these roles are adhered to.

Symbols have meaning to the individual if the person has experienced the meaning of the symbols. When a male who has been deeply involved in institutionalized sport is asked why he plays basketball, he usually responds: "Because I like to win." When he is asked whether he enjoys playing basketball, the answer is: "When I win." Isn't it enough he plays his best? His answer would be: "No one wants to be a loser." Women tend to respond: "I like basketball." "I am satisfied if I did my best." These are generalizations, of course, but men and women have had different experiences when it comes to organized athletics. Athletics mean different things to men than they do to women. Words associated with athletics have different meanings because of the different experiences.

Socialization: Learning the Rules of the Game

A social system develops the skills and talents that the system needs to have developed in people. Direct instruction, demonstration, rewards and punishments are used for this purpose. Each new situation requires learning new rules. Children are socialized through a process of stages until they finally internalize the rules. In this society, girls do not fully develop the idea that they are "not intelligent" and nonproductive until they get to high school. That is when they begin to score lower than boys on a few intellectual tasks. Weisstein states:

> It is no use to talk about women being different but equal; all of the tests I can think of have a "good" outcome and a "bad" outcome. In the light of social expectations about women, what is surprising is not that women end up where society expects they will; what is surprising is that little girls don't get the message that they are supposed to be stupid until high school. (6)

How girls get the message is evident to all: school books, television, comics, novels, movies, language, clothing, toys, games and sports are all designed to get this message across. Finally the girls and boys have acquired the stereotyped types of behavior which match the expectations. Weisstein goes on to say that if women "know their place, which is in the home, they are really quite lovable, happy, childlike, loving creatures" (6).

This has been a very simplified attempt to summarize some of the concepts of sociology with regard to culture, language, and socialization. What are the implications for the coaches and players in the women's sports program?

Looking at American culture, one can ask: Is there a place for women's sports in American culture? Is it a place of high priority? Some sports certainly are valued for women, but probably no sport assumes the same position for women as for men. Sport is not a high-priority item for women. It is for many men. Basketball, most team sports, and many other forms of institutionalized sport are a major part of the male culture. Madge Phillips summarizes the writing of Ann Battle-Sister by saying that "women do not have an independent culture and that they do not participate freely in male culture. Women then are trying to build a female culture complete with counter-institutions" (4). The question must be asked: Will sport ever assume the position of value for women that it should in the "male" culture?

If women try to participate freely in the male culture, assuming for a moment that this were possible, what does this imply? Using basketball as the example, this sport gives man a chance to test his masculinity. Strength, speed, endurance and skill are clearly visible in the performance. In the male culture, basketball is used as entertainment. The show goes on sometimes at the expense of the participant. Basketball is a game where rules are changed to make it more enjoyable for the spectators. More and more body contact is being allowed because that is what the people come to see. Players are bought with scholarships; players are to work hard at the game. Basketball is serious business. Recruiting is a must for college teams and even extends to many high school teams as well. There is little place in organized basketball where the players are encouraged to enjoy the process of the game, for only the final product is glorified and valued. The rules are clearly drawn and, within the framework of the game, it is acceptable to foul to prevent a shot. This is called "strategy." It is sometimes met with approval if one breaks a rule and does not get caught. The role of the coach, the player, the recruiter, the official and the fan are well established. The models are there for all to see.

If women try to participate in the male sport subculture rather than develop their own subculture, will they not continue to remain in an unequal position in terms of number of participants, facilities, time for play and practice, money for equipment and personnel? Women cannot compete against men in events where physical strength is a factor in the outcome of the contest. Even when women play against women, if they remain in the male sport subculture, they will be measured against the standards set by men. If they fall short in this evaluation, money, time and space will continue to be allocated on the basis of the ones who measure up to this standard, the men.

For the first time in the lives of many girls and women, females are becoming involved in a much more competitive sporting situation. State tournaments, league play, more pressure to win, gate receipts, scholarships recruiting all are becoming part of the women's sport scene. Some women are using the male model and trying to mold women's sport according to the male subculture. The situation is now at hand where women must make the critical decision: shall they use the male model for women's sport? shall they accept the male values? shall they assume the male roles? or shall they develop their own models to be emulated by girls and women. Shall they establish a subculture for women's athletics? Women athletes have been shown to have doubts about their own sexual identity and role which cause them to feel a great deal of stress. This is understandable when they model themselves after the male coach and male athlete. What else can they do when there are no female models in a female subculture to follow?

It is proposed that a counterculture for women's sports be developed. Sport then can be one of many ventures where girls and women can fulfill themselves, where achievement training can replace non-achievement training, where girls can develop feelings of self-confidence and usefulness, and where girls will not be afraid to say, "I *can*," where women can express their femininity, where women can be compared to women in their skill execution. Sport can be a place where a girl can experience who she is and what she is, where she can learn what she is capable of achieving. Sport can be viewed without overemphasis on winning, but with winning being a part of the game. Sport can be a place where all participants can be winners, where losing the contest does not demean and degrade. Sport can maintain its integrity and value for the participant and not be used solely as a show or a spectacle. If such a subculture develops, sport can become an acceptable and sought-after avenue for women. Norms and roles will be developed that will be acceptable for women in the eyes of both men and women.

Can it work? Women's tennis and women's golf are examples where women found that they could not enter into the male sport subculture on an equal basis with the men. They completely separated themselves from their male counterparts, and the results speak for themselves. This separation may be the forerunner of the women's sport subculture.

The development of a sport subculture for women will require that the leaders in this program truly view women as worthy of respect, as human beings equal in their human-ness to men. These leaders will have to be people who can appreciate well-executed skills, beauty in movement, the joy of the action. Those leaders will have to establish themselves as the role models, the ones to be emulated by the little girls who are searching for models with which to identify. These leaders will take their place beside the woman doctor, the woman lawyer, the woman professional as representing a place where women can assume a social and economic role equal to men.

REFERENCES

1. Broverman, I. et al. "Sex Role Stereotypes and Clinical Judgments of Mental Health." *Journal of Consulting and Clinical Psychology* 34: 1-7, 1970.
2. Griffin, Patricia S. "What's a Nice Girl Like You Doing in a Profession Like This?" *Quest* 19: 96-100, Jan. 1973.
3. Metheny, Eleanor. "Symbolic Forms of Movement; The Feminine Image in Sports." In *Connotations of Movement in Sport and Dance,* pp. 43-56. Dubuque, Iowa: William C. Brown Co., 1965.
4. Phillips, Madge. "Women in Sport: The Impact of Society." In *DGWS Research Reports: Women in Sports,* pp. 5-14. Washington, D.C.: American Association for Health, Physical Education and Recreation, 1971.
5. Sadler, William A., Jr. "Competition Out of Bounds: Sport in American Life." *Quest* 19: 124-132, Jan. 1973.
6. Weisstein, Naomi. "Psychology Constructs the Female." In *Sociology in the World Today,* pp. 53-56. Reading, Mass.: Addison-Wesley Publishing Co., 1971.

Women Athletic Trainers

Holly Wilson

HOLLY WILSON is Athletic Trainer in the Women's
Physical Education Department at Indiana State
University, Terre Haute, one of the very few women
Certified Athletic Trainers.

Athletic training is the care and prevention of athletic injuries. Sixty percent of the trainer's time should be spent in preventing injuries. Prevention involves not only taping but conditioning as well. Conditioning is the more important aspect. Immediate first aid and rehabilitation are the two steps in the proper care of an injury.

The entrance of women into the field of athletic training has been slow, but now it is beginning to gain momentum. The cause, of course, is the rapid growth and development of the interscholastic and intercollegiate athletic programs for girls and women. Administrators realize that a need exists for someone to care for the injured athletes. After all, athletics expose the women to many of the same hazards the men athletics encounter in their sports. Rapid movement, change of direction, starting and stopping are just a few of the hazards inherent in sports. The injury incidence in women's athletics may never be comparable to the men's, but the fact remains that injuries do occur. It is the responsibility of administrators to provide for the welfare of the female athlete.

Today, although the woman trainer would have difficulty in finding a position as a trainer, she is beginning to be recognized as a vital member of the physical education faculty. In a recent survey of administrators of women's physical education departments in colleges and universities throughout the United States, 54 of 73 felt there was a definite need for women trainers. There were three main reasons for opposition: the budget would not allow for a trainer; first aiders were just as competent; and injuries were low in number and minor. It is to be hoped that in the near future more positions will open up for women trainers.

Every day, more and more coaches and students seek out means of acquiring a background in training. They attend workshops and clinics. Is this the best answer to meet the need for proper health care for injured athletes? No, but for now it has to suffice, for the coach or student with a basic knowledge of training techniques is better than no one. Women athletes deserve the same professionally trained personnel as the men — certified athletic trainers.

Today, there are 24 schools in the United States that offer athletic training curricula which have been approved by the National Athletic Trainers

Association. Of those 24, possibly only five accept women into their programs. The schools are Ball State University in Muncie, Indiana; Indiana State University in Terre Haute; Western Illinois University in Macomb; West Chester State in Westchester, Pennsylvania; and the University of Montana in Missoula. Indiana State is the only school that offers supervision by both men and women trainers. It also has an approved graduate curriculum in athletic training, and the Women's Physical Education Department offers a graduate assistantship in athletic training. Indiana State's undergraduate curriculum consists of an interdepartmental specialization of 24 hours. Classes within the specialization cover not only the diagnosis and treatment of injuries but also nutrition, insurance coverage, legal liability, rehabilitation, and conditioning. In addition to the theory classes, the student trainer spends 3 semesters working in the training room to practice the skills she has learned. The student may fulfill the entrance requirements for physical therapy school at the same time that she is completing the specialization. She need only take 8 hours each of chemistry and physics.

The other means by which a student may acquire a background in athletic training include: enrollment in an introductory course in athletic training at her own school or nearby university; completion of the Cramer's Student Trainer Course offered by Cramer Products, Inc., one of the leading manufacturers of athletic training products; serving an apprenticeship under a trainer.

For the coach to acquire an adequate background in athletic training, her best bet would be to combine an apprenticeship with the theoretical knowledge gained in an introductory athletic-training course.

The advantages of having a trainer are that the trainer: frees the coach from worrying about injuries while she is thinking about strategy; provides well-rounded health care for the athlete (potential injuries may be eliminated through proper conditioning, treatment, rehabilitation and strapping); helps eliminate the injuries of a sympathy-seeking, injury-prone athlete; and takes over responsibility of injury care.

Once an individual with a background in athletic training has been identified, setting up a training program is not without problems. First, the individual may have trouble gaining acceptance by many of her colleagues. Suspicion stems from the fact that a trainer was never needed before, so one isn't needed now; however, women never competed in athletics on a level comparable with that of today. Secondly, the trainer may find it difficult, if not impossible, to establish rapport with some coaches. Without such rapport, the welfare of the athlete is often at stake. Without the coaches' mutual consent of who should be benched due to an injury, the athletic training program cannot survive. It might be wise to keep in mind that the injured athlete going at half speed may be more of a handicap to the team than a blessing.

Concerning the future, every day high school and college students ask questions about the opportunities for women in athletic training. When these women are ready to seek positions as trainers, I hope there will be positions available. Presently, I do not know of any university, college, or high school which desires to hire a certified woman trainer, but more women students at both the high school and college level are being given opportunities to explore the field of athletic training. Many men are opening up their training rooms to the women athletes. This is true at the University of Iowa, Ithaca College, and West Chester State, to name a few of the schools. Several high schools have done the same. In talking with the trainers, the only problem in switching to the co-ed room was the necessity to change the dress code. Men were required to wear shorts. Other than that, many felt that the presence of women introduced respect into the training room. Once the men got used to the new situation they even let the woman tape them.

There are many problems associated with the change such as inaccessibility of the room, the involvement of the men's trainers with their work, and individual problems unique to each situation. Rather than discuss the merits of opening up the men's training room to women, therefore, I will focus on the set-up of a modest training room for the women athletes. This isn't difficult to do and can be accomplished on a very limited budget. All that is needed is a spare room or even a corner of the locker room, providing there is a locked storage cabinet available for supplies.

Training Room Equipment

The room should be well lit and large enough to accommodate at least a table, a storage cabinet, a small refrigerator, some benches or chairs, and perhaps a desk. At Indiana State, the faculty kitchen was converted into a very adequate training room, although it could well have been larger. The room was ideal because it already contained a sink, a refrigerator, and cabinets. If at all possible, running water should be available in the room.

The refrigerator is the only needed modality. There is also an infra-red lamp, compliments of the men, but it has been used very rarely in the last five years. Any refrigerator will do, but it should have a large freezer, the larger the better. It is used to store ice packs, ice cubes and ice cups for ice massage, besides the Kool Aid salt solution to prevent heat exhaustion. I believe entirely in using ice for the rehabilitation of any injury. Actually ice is the only modality I can afford. What women's department can spare $400-600 for a deep heat modality? Besides, ice has its advantages; it is a pain reliever, a vasoconstrictor, and a muscle relaxer. It would be far wiser to pick up a second-hand refrigerator. GAA's and WAA's often come up with money-making projects, or one of the community organizations might be eager to invest in a worthwhile project. Another necessity is a locked storage cabinet, even if the training room is a separate room. Elastic wraps and rolls of tape have a tendency to disappear.

Two pieces of optional furniture are the desk and table for supplies. The desk serves as a storage place for records. It is necessary to keep records of all injuries and treatments, not only to justify the training program, but also for insurance needs. At Indiana State, three forms are completed on every injury: the injury form which is a carbon triplicate, a detailed description of the injury, and a running log of treatments and injuries. The injury form is an excellent method of keeping track of supplies. Elastic wraps, towels, and crutches used in the first-aid treatment of an injury are recorded on the form. One copy is given to the main office, one copy to the equipment room, and the other remains in the training room. The injured athlete has three locations where she can return the supplies. If she fails to do so by the end of the semester, she will be unable to register until the supplies are paid for or returned.

The only pieces of exercise equipment in the Indiana State women's training room are an improvised knee machine, an improvised ankle exerciser, and several disc weights. Both exercise machines have proven to be quite useful, and they are inexpensive to build, especially when compared to the price of the originals which range from $200 to $400 apiece. All that is needed to make the two machines functional are some disc weights, which are relatively cheap. Perhaps the industrial arts class or the physical plant would build the two machines. If not, school facilities can be used: the swimming pool can be a whirlpool where the buoyancy of the water eliminates some of the pain associated with the movement; the track can be used for jogging. Injured athletes should be encouraged to ride bicycles to rehabilitate ankle and knee injuries. If weights are needed, sand bags can be made or plastic bottles filled with sand. Another suggestion is to use an empty fruit can with the top and bottom removed, one end crushed to fit on the toe of a shoe, and a brick put in the other end. Or simply, a disc weight may be taped to the sole of an old tennis shoe.

As far as supplies for the training room, the equantity needed will depend on the scope of the program and the budget. A modest training room could be stocked with $100-$200. The most expensive item would be tape.

Necessary Supplies

A list of necessities would include:

1. Tape, 1½" white porous. 1½" is the most suitable width for women athletes. It may be split to 1" or even ½" depending on the need.
2. Tape adherent. A quart of liquid is more economical than the spray can. It is painted on with a brush.
3. Tape remover.
4. Non-sterile gauze rolls or sponges, to protect the lace and heel areas when strapping.
5. Bandage scissors (5½" and 7¼") and tape cutters.
6. Vinyl foam rather than sponge rubber to pad bruises.
7. Elastic wraps, 3" and 4", for compression after a sprain or strain and to hold analgesic packs in place.
8. Analgesic-counterirritant for analgesic (heat) packs, a mild, water-soluble brand, if possible.
9. Combine (cotton padding) for analgesic packs, or substitutes such as pieces of old towel or Pampers diapers. To prevent the analgesic from soaking into the elastic wrap, the towel or combine should be covered with a plastic wrap.
10. Cold packs if ice is not available, good for trips. Companies are now manufacturing reusable packs which could be a money saver.
11. Band aids, 1" and extra large.
12. First-aid cream.
13. Sterile gauze pads.
14. Alcohol or a substitute that doesn't burn.
15. Hydrogen peroxide for cleaning out abrasions.
16. Cotton-tipped applicators.
17. Tongue depressors to use as finger splints (slightly curved or straight), and spreaders for analgesic and vaseline.

18. Vaseline, a lubricant to prevent blisters.
19. Ice jug. A good jug costing $10-$12 will outlast the styrofoam type.
20. Ammonia inhalants.
21. Safety pins and rubber bands always come in handy.
22. Training kit. A fishing tackle box might be used.

Some of the leading manufacturers of athletic training supplies are: Cramer Products, Inc. in Gardner, Kansas; School Health Supply in Addison, Illinois; Johnson and Johnson in New Brunswick, New Jersey; and Bike Division of Kendall Company in Wellesley Hills, Massachusetts. If at all possible, it is wiser to deal directly with a local sporting goods store or a surgical supply company in a local town. Sometimes discounts can be arranged even when a small quantity of an item is purchased.

Injuries and Treatment

Common injuries are blisters, ankle and knee sprains and shin splints. Blisters are simply friction burns that usually occur during the early part of the season. They are easier to prevent than cure. A skin toughener (tape adherent) should not be used on the soles of the feet to toughen them up; it usually results in the formation of calluses and eventually blisters. The most comon causes of blisters are shoes and socks that are too big or too small. Shoes that are too big slide, and those too small pinch. Rough spots on the shoes, such as the eyelets and the stitching, may also irritate the skin. Wetness from perspiration of the feet increases friction. In the socks, the seams or balls of lint can cause blisters. Socks that are too big wrinkle, and they pinch if they are too small.

Blisters may be prevented in many ways:
1. Filing down calluses with an emory board until they are smooth. This is easier when the feet have been soaked in water.
2. Applying a lubricant such as vaseline to the soles of the feet and problem areas.
3. Shaking foot powder in the shoes to combat wetness.
4. If there is a hot spot, taking off the shoe and sock to cool the area. It is better yet to stick feet in a pan of ice water. Before putting on the shoe and sock, a lubricant is applied to the area. At the USCSC Volleyball Camp at Illinois State in August 1972, the most handicapping "injury" was the blister. The participants did not want to take the time to cool off their feet, so they suffered the consequences

—blisters. Not until late in the camp did one brave suffering player try the cold water soak, and then its use spread like wildfire. Those women were practicing approximately 3-5 hours a day and sometimes 6 or 7, but through the use of the cold water soaks, the problem was finally controlled.

5. Wearing two pairs of socks, thin cotton next to the skin and thick wool on the outside to absorb perspiration.
6. Changing socks daily and washing them frequently using a fabric softener.
7. Wearing socks wrong side out to eliminate the seams.
8. Wearing tube socks to eliminate the heel seam (but then the heel may slide).
9. Wearing properly fitted shoes and socks.
10. Breaking in new shoes slowly, before the big game.
11. If innersoles are used, purchasing a good brand.

Prevention is the key word. An athletic training text should be checked for the proper treatment of blisters. The conservative treatment is recommended in which the blister is padded against further assault. There is little danger of infection if the skin is not punctured or cut. Of course, a school's first-aid policy will dictate what can and cannot be done.

Another related "injury" is the rip in gymnastics. Usually a piece of rough skin, a callus, is caught on the bar which results in the tearing off of several layers of skin. Once the skin has been ripped, there is little one can do except pad the area and protect it from further assault. Tape handgrips are applied directly to the skin for new rips and as a preventative. Leather handgrips are worn over the tape ones. To prevent rips, the callused areas are filed down until they are smooth, and then vaseline applied to keep the area moist.

An ankle sprain results from a lateral or medial twisting of the foot. 85% of the time, the sole is turned inward. Therefore, damage is to the ligaments on the lateral side. The ankle should be checked to see if pain exists below, in front of, or behind the ankle bone (malleolus). If it does, damage involves the ligaments. A fracture may be present if the pain is localized along the shaft of the tibia or fibula. There is a possibility of a bone chip if pain occurs along the border of the ankle bone. A wet elastic wrap should be applied to the injured area as well as the area directly above and below. The wrap should be wet to speed up the conduction of the cold to the tissue. The ice pack can either be a chemical pack or a wet towel full of ice cubes. It is placed directly over the injury and held in place with a dry elastic wrap. The foot should be elevated above the hip for 30-60 minutes, or immersed in a bucket of ice slush as long as possible. The foot can be warmed by taking it out of the slush and then reimmersed. Total immersion time should be at least 30 minutes. If a fracture is suspected, the joint is splinted above and below the fracture, and crutches provided. Arrangements should be made to transport the athlete to the Health Center. First-aid procedures of the school should be followed if the trainer is a high school teacher.

A knee injury often occurs when the foot is planted and the individual attempts to change directions (cutting) or is hit. If pain is localized along the joint line, it may indicate damage to the cartilage; however, cartilage tears rarely occur on first time sprains. Ligaments are involved if the pain is above or below the joint line, approximately three inches below on the medial side, or if the pain is localized within the knee joint. Pressure, ice and elevation are applied for 30-90 minutes. After the ice treatment, the knee is wrapped in a dry elastic wrap, and the athlete is given crutches if needed. Immediate swelling and toe walking, an attempt to splint the knee, are indications of a severe injury. If crutches are not needed, the athlete is cautioned to walk as normally as possible, even if she must go slower, to avoid straining the back.

When dealing with an injury to a joint, the bad is always compared with the good. It is very difficult to determine the severity of an injury without such a comparison. Previous injury makes the task even more difficult.

Shin splints is characterized by pain in the lower leg usually along the medial border, but it may be anterior or posterior. The mechanism is unknown and for this reason it is the plague of the coach. Some of the probable causes include: a change in playing surface, weak arches, a change in shoe type, muscle imbalance in the lower leg, overuse (doing too much too soon), and lack of conditioning of the lower leg muscles.

Many trainers think that shin splints is progressive. It starts as a muscle strain of the tibialis anterior or posterior. If nothing is done to alleviate the problem, the interosseous membrane becomes involved. Then the muscles pull away from the periosteum at their attachments. Finally the bones can no longer compensate, and a green stick fracture occurs. At Indiana State, treatment for shin splints consists of ice massage, strapping the arch, analgesic packs and rehabilitation exercises consisting of inversion, eversion and dorsiflexion isometrics and gastrocnemius stretching. Ice massage is the rubbing of ice cups or cubes directly over the skin of the painful area or injury for 8-10 minutes. Following the application of ice, three minutes of exercise are carried out. This procedure of ice rubbing followed by exercise is repeated three times. Ice massage is used before the rehabilitation of any joint or muscle injury.

To prevent shin splints, the athlete should wear a good pair of shoes with good arch supports, strengthen the lower leg muscles by doing inversion, eversion and dorsiflexion isometrics, and stretch out the gastrocnemius (Achilles tendon). When jogging, alternate a counterclockwise lap with a clockwise lap to avoid placing stress on one leg only.

Rehabilitation, which is perhaps the most important preventative of re-injury, has been overlooked by many coaches and athletes. To understand the need for rehabilitation, one must consider what has happened to the tissue during trauma. During a sprain, the joint structure has been disrupted, the ligaments have been either stretched or torn. Consequently, the joint is not as stable because, once ligaments have been stretched, they remain in the elongated position. Therefore, it is necessary to compensate for the loss of the ligamentous stability by strengthening the muscles that cross the joint. For example, following a knee sprain, the athlete should strengthen the quadriceps, the hamstrings, and the gastrocnemius. When rehabilitating a joint or muscle, it is important to regain the range of motion and then the strength.

Taping never takes the place of rehabilitation. The athlete should not be allowed to participate in practice or competition until the muscles are strong enough to withstand the stress of the sport. At Indiana State, slips are sent to the coaches stating the activities that the athlete is fit to engage in, usually on the recommendation of the team physician, and an inactivity list is posted. Of course, neither will work without the cooperation of the coach.

Another area of concern is game preparation. For games, a trainer's kit and ice should be available on the floor or field. The kit should be packed the night before with those items previously mentioned as essential. If there is not adequate storage space in the freezer for ice packs, ice cubes can be obtained at the dorm or cafeteria the morning of the game. The ice packs should be made in dry towels and stored, along with the wet elastic wrap, in the ice jug. If an injury occurs, the towel is wet, and the wet elastic wrap and the ice pack are applied. If some of the packs aren't used, they can be stored in the freezer until the next game. Tape, tape adherent and a tape cutter must be available, for the trainer might be called upon to make some adjustment to a tape job. The phone numbers of the doctor or Health Center, ambulance and fire department should be handy. Taping is scheduled 45-60 minutes before the team is due on the floor for warm-up; the time will depend on how fast the trainer tapes and the number of athletes that need taping.

Two good athletic training texts are:

Modern Principles of Athletic Training by Klafs and Arnheim. This is perhaps the most complete text on athletic training and is a valuable reference. It is published by C. V. Mosby.

The Dixonary of Athletic Training by Spike Dixon. It is one of the best taping manuals available today, and may be obtained by writing directly to Spike Dixon, 119 N. Jefferson, Bloomington, Indiana 47401.

A recently published text that covers the physiological, psychological and sociological aspects of coaching the female athlete is *The Female Athlete* by Klafs and Lyon. The publisher is C. V. Mosby.

ALSO AVAILABLE FROM AAHPER

DGWS RESEARCH REPORTS I

Women in Sports, the first in the DGWS research series, covers the teaching, coaching, physiological, and psychosocial aspects of the subject, with emphasis on research implications and applications. It reports results of research in physical education and related fields for use by those working with girls and women involved in competitive sports or those learning and performing motor skills. The book can be easily understood by the person without a background in research and statistics.

DGWS RESEARCH REPORTS II

The second volume in a series of research reports designed to provide the practitioner with scientific evidence on which to base decisions relating to programs of physical activity and athletics for girls and women. The content is applicable to all levels, and can be easily understood by the person without a background in research and statistics. Some of the specific topics covered in this volume are femininity and achievement, female aggression, familial influence, stress conditioning, ability prediction, and iron deficiency.

PHILOSOPHY AND STANDARDS IN GIRLS AND WOMEN'S SPORTS

An indispensable guide for those who administer, lead, and participate in sports programs for girls and women. Covers the nature, value, implementation, conduct and evaluation of sports programs as they relate to the leader, the administrator, the official and the participant. Includes DGWS policy statements and guidelines on interscholastic and intercollegiate competition.

RESEARCH METHODS IN HEALTH, PHYSICAL EDUCATION, AND RECREATION

An up-to-date, authoritative reference and basic textbook written by nationally known research specialists. Presented in clear, direct style and set in easy-to-read type, it deals with all phases of research — from selecting a problem to the final writing of the report. An invaluable tool for the experienced researcher and teacher of graduate courses, as well as the student working on his first project. It is indexed and has extensive bibliographies for each subject treated.

CURRENT SPORTS MEDICINE ISSUES

An authoritative treatment of current issues in sports safety and sports medicine, prepared especially for physical educators, coaches, athletic directors, trainers, and safety educators. It capitalizes on the emphasis of the First National Sports Safety Congress in February, 1973, with articles appearing under eight major categories: the medical aspects of safety in sports; product safety; educational standards in sports medicine; athletic injury reporting; the female athlete; legal considerations in the conduct of athletic programs; the supervision of sports programs; and government interest in sports safety. Published as the 1973 issue of AAPHER's *Annual Safety Education Review.*

SPORTS GUIDES
The Division for Girls and Women's Sports publishes guides, with articles and rules, for the following sports or activities, on an annual or biennial basis: aquatics, archery, golf, basketball, bowling, fencing, field hockey, lacrosse, gymnastics, outing activities, winter sports, soccer, speedball, flag football, track and field, softball, tennis, badminton, squash, and volleyball. Separate rulebooks, technique charts, selected articles, and scorebooks are also available for certain sports.

AIAW HANDBOOK
A revision of the handbook of policies and operating procedures of the Association for Intercollegiate Athletics for Women. Contains statements on the structure, purposes, and membership of AIAW; policies and procedures for AIAW National Championships; and interim regulations for awarding of financial aid and for recruitment. Revised 1973.

AIAW DIRECTORY
The 1973 edition, listing officers, representatives, regions, and member institutions of the Association for Intercollegiate Athletics for Women. Also includes information on 19 sports in which intercollegiate programs for women are offered, showing which of these are offered at each member school. The appendix gives schedules of AIAW National Championships in seven sports and AIAW National JC/CC Championships in three sports, with a listing of sports advisory committees for both, and selected references.

FOR A CURRENT PRICE LIST AND ORDER INSTRUCTIONS, WRITE:
AAHPER, 1201 16th Street, N.W., Washington, D.C. 20036